Tax Secrets Made Simple

Edward W. Cotney

*"In America, there are two tax systems:
one for the informed and one for the
uninformed. Both are Legal"*

Judge Learned Hand

All stories in this book are based on actual experiences. In some cases, the names and details have been changed to protect the privacy of the people involved. Some materials may be affected by changes in laws or in the interpretations of such laws since the manuscript for this book was completed. For that reason, the accuracy and completeness of such information and the opinions based thereon are not guaranteed. In addition, state and local laws, or procedural rules may have a material impact on the general recommendations made by the author, and the strategies outlined in this book may not be suitable for every individual. Anyone planning to act in any of the areas this book describes should seek professional advice as would be prudent and advisable under their given circumstances.

ISBN 978-1983664212

Olympus Tax, Business and Insurance Solutions, Inc.

Edward W. Cotney

4600 Roseville Road, Ste 260

Sacramento, CA 95660

www.OlympusTax.com

Edward W. Cotney

www.OlympusTax.com

Mr. Cotney is the founder of Olympus Tax, Business and Insurance Solutions, Inc. He is considered an expert on tax issues and strategies relating to income tax planning, asset sales, mergers, and retirement planning alternatives.

Raised in Alabama (Roll Tide), he joined the US Air Force to travel and obtain an education. After his retirement in 1998, he graduated from the Professional Mentoring Program to become a Family Wealth Counselor. Since then, he successfully designed hundreds of wealth enhancement strategies to reduce and in many cases, eliminate multiple layers of taxation.

Lauded by many for his ability to make complex strategies easy to understand, he often provides continuing education for professional advisors and organizations of every type.

His passion is helping families discover their "why" by helping them make this a better place to live.

To my wife Laura and our children, Joe and Chrysten.

You are my greatest joy!

Acknowledgements

As I reflect on my past, without question, this country boy has been blessed beyond imagination. Countless people have poured into me with love, training, mentorship and above all, wisdom. Although my name appears as the author of this book, I owe a huge debt of gratitude to the following people and I am certain I have omitted many.

Barbara Bradbury, Barbara Jennings, Barbara Tackett, EA, Charles Schultz, Esq., David Shafer, Esq., Ed Dean, Esq., Eric Sams, CFP, George Graziano, CPA, Helen Justice, J. T. Houk, JD, PhD., James Hunt, USAF, James Cunningham, Jr, Esq., Jay Link, Jeff Hays, USAF, John Graham, USAF, John Tidgewell, PhD, John Knowlton, Esq., Kate Swain-Beeman, Esq., Kevin Wagner, USAF, Kim Rhinehelder, C. Kipp Wordell, Esq., Larry Burkett, Lori Humphrey, Mario Buda, USAF, Micheal L. Meyer, Esq., CPA, Micheal Bennett, Esq., Mike Parker, USAF, Mitchell Caldwell, Neil Beeman, CPA, Phil Bodine, Randy Roth, EA, Robert Keebler, CPA, Roger Minor, Esq., Ron Blue, Ronny Jennings, Russell Snapp, Sam Bellicini, Esq., Steve McCormick, CPA, Steve Morgan, Steve and Vicki Orsillo, Steve Oshins, Esq., Keith Springer, Stuart Furman, Esq., Todd Humphrey, Tom Ray, Esq., Wayne Handley, US Navy, James Higham, USAF, and Mike Montgomery, MD, US Navy.

Special thanks to this medical team for saving my life three times in 2015-2017. Barry Schneidewind, DO, Ryan Bennett, MD, Amer Khan, MD, Jan Babiszewski, MD, Michael Chin, MD, Madhu Jodhani, MD, Ranganth Pathak, MD, Craig Glaiberman, MD, Jon Marsh, DO, Michael Wilkerson, MD, Michael Fahey, MD, Anthony Gravin, DPT, Gary Sumner, DDS and Sutter Health Roseville, California.

Table of Contents

Preface: Toward the Unknown… 1

Chapter 1: Your Report Card 3

Chapter 2: Rich verses Wealthy...6

Chapter 3: Ownership vs. Control...9

Chapter 4: The Four Phases of Money...11

Chapter 5: Maximum Wealth Control – Tax Free Sale of Business or Appreciated Assets...14

Chapter 6: Research and Development Tax Credits............................18

Chapter 7: Export Tax Benefits / IC-DISC 23

Chapter 8: Cost Segregation Study 25

Chapter 9: 1031 Exchanges Are Tax Bombs for the Wealthy! 27

Chapter 10: Finding Strong Advisors...29

Chapter 11: Charitable Tax Planning Basics 32

Chapter 12: The Charitable Gift Annuity – One of my favorites! 37

Chapter 13: Blended Gifts – Part Sale / Part Charitable Gift.............42

Chapter 14: Better Than an IRA or 401K? The Retirement Uni-Trust! 46

Chapter 15: To Roth or Not to Roth, that is the question? 52

Chapter 16: Will Your Traditional IRA Actually Get to Your Heirs? 55

Chapter 17: The "Give It Away Twice Trust" 60

Chapter 18: Income in Respect of a Decedent (IRD)........................65

Chapter 19: Qualified Plan Tax Strip Out..68

Chapter 20: Business Owner Tax Credits and Additional Deductions (CCTC / NEC / WOTC)...71

Chapter 21: Game Over – End of Life..77

Chapter 22: Summary – Call to Action..82

Preface
Toward the Unknown...

"I am not worried about what I know about taxes or wealth, rather, it is what I do not know." Edward W. Cotney

My objective in this book is to share twenty years of tax secrets many believe are beyond their grasp. Be assured, the tax code and tax rates will continue to change. This book will focus on structure, strategy and timing, which is why you should not be overly concerned about tax percentages.

Why did you purchase this book? Chances are, your accountant, attorney, banker, financial planner, insurance agent or realtor is fearful you will start asking the following questions which they cannot answer.

1. Show me how to reduce my income tax by thirty to sixty percent for the rest of my life.

2. Show me how to avoid paying any capital gains tax for the rest of my life.

3. Show me how to avoid paying any gift tax for the rest of my life.

4. Show me how to avoid paying any estate tax upon my death.

If any one of your advisors can show you how to address any two of the four questions above, that advisor is among the less than one percent who can be considered a pro-active tax and wealth planner. For the remaining ninety nine percent of you, use this book to educate yourselves and your advisors and stop over paying your taxes!

Sadly, many of your advisors are trapped in positions where providing you pro-active tax and wealth advice is prohibited due to errors and omissions insurance, company policy, regulatory compliance, lack of training, and the excuses go on and on. However; if you approach them with the concept, they will be forced into a position of participation, because you initiated the discussion. Often, they will have little, if any, experience with advanced tax planning, which means they will not be able to weigh in with any level of expertise.

Most advisors when challenged with a technical question will respond with "That is probably not a good strategy for you at this time". What that statement really means is "I have no clue what you are talking about, but I do not want to look weak in front of you"! One easy way to find out what an advisor does or does not know about advanced tax planning concepts is to ask them to put their objection to your proposed tax strategy in writing. Since they can't, you have gotten your answer. If this is your most trusted advisor, ask them to help you find a qualified person who can opine to the solution you seek.

My objective by writing this book is to empower you with tools, whether your income is $50,000.00 or $50,000,000.00 a year, to reduce, and in many cases, eliminate various layers of tax you are currently paying. This book has many tools for employees, self-employed persons and business owners. For your reading pleasure, I have tried to keep boring, technical data, tax code and court case references to a minimum.

For you to obtain the most benefit from this book, I ask that you forget about all of the investment, insurance, trust, banking, real estate and accounting seminars you have attended to date. I ask that you give me a clean, white sheet of paper to write a better story to proactively build and protect your wealth, reduce your taxes for life, and provide greater benefits for you, your family and your community.

This book will cause you to critically question the bulk of what you have been taught to do with money, wealth and tax. By the end of this book, I am hopeful you will rethink your current plan and implement structure, strategy and timing processes to more effectively accomplish your short and long-term goals. If you are waiting on your advisors to show you how to pay less tax for life, you will remain a member of the ninety-nine percent club who overpay their taxes and die waiting for that advice!

Chapter 1
Your Report Card

Like it or not, December 31 is a tax deadline we race against every year. The race is to make money, create expenses or deductions, and to pay the least amount of tax due on April 17. For some reason, we measure our success by the amount of money we get to keep, after paying a tax computed by constantly changing tax laws, deductions, credits and expenses. Simply, it is an annual race where the rules always change.

The rules of the race are contained in over 75,000 pages of Federal Tax Code. Sadly, you may be using about 100 of those pages to your benefit. Contained in the remainder of that wonderful book of great secrets, separately under Title 26 of the United States Code (USC), you will discover opportunities that may seem too good to be true. For those who look at new concepts as too good to be true, you will be challenged and rewarded by reading this book.

The Best Kept Tax Secret is Schedule A, Line 19. By now you have either pulled out your prior return or used the Internet to find a 1040 form at the IRS.gov web site. As your eyes scroll down Schedule A, Medical and Dental Expenses, Taxes You Paid, Interest You Paid, Gifts to Charity…..add lines 16 through 18 and write the amount on line 19 to the far right side of the page, your brain has immediately jumped to what it thinks it knows about Line 19 and you are dead wrong. Sorry, but there is no way to make this easy for you to understand other than to state the obvious. If you knew how to effectively and efficiently use this line to significantly reduce your annual income tax burden by thirty to sixty percent per year, you would have been doing it all along. In this book, I will consistently prove to you why this line, and many more planning tools, is the most powerful planning opportunity at your discretion and why you and your trusted advisors are failing to use this to maximize your personal wealth.

You were taught at a very early age in life to donate funds to worthy causes. Later in your working years, you continued using that personal virtue of giving. Your CPA/EA taught you to claim those donations on your 1040. In fact, most Americans are shocked to learn this is one of the best kept tax secrets used by many high net worth individuals who publicly state they are in the eighteen percent income tax bracket. The same tax code that helps millionaires and billionaires pay minimal tax can do the same for you - once you break free from what you don't know.

Let's begin with a simple exercise. Assume your tax advisor has claimed every possible expense, deduction, mortgage interest, contributions to qualified plans, and you are sitting on a taxable adjusted income (report card) where you made $500,000.00 of taxable income (page 2, line 43 of your 1040). There are a few minor tax deductions before you get to line 63 for a small group of taxpayers, but what if you had used Schedule A, Line 19 to your maximum tax benefit?

Since the tax code allows us to contribute up to sixty percent of our taxable adjusted income (cash) to tax exempt charitable causes, technically, we could have donated up to $300,000.00 of cash and claimed that amount on Schedule A, Line 19. Which means, our new taxable adjusted income is greatly reduced instead of $500,000.00. BEFORE YOUR UNTRAINED BRAIN JUMPS TO A WRONG CONCLUSION, what if that $300,000.00 had been contributed to a Charitable Retirement Plan to provide you a generous income stream when you are ready to retire?

If you were a W-2 employee, let's assume you max funded your traditional IRA with $5,500.00 (the current year of this writing is 2017). Let's assume the taxpayer is age 42 today. Let's assume his or her income and tax status remain the same.

If his or her goals are to significantly reduce their income tax and develop a substantial retirement portfolio, which of the two retirement plans above will accomplish that goal assuming the taxpayer desires to retire at age 62?

The Traditional IRA was funded every year for the next twenty years with $5,500.00. In twenty years, there should be a corpus of $110,000.00 plus the deferred growth.

The Charitable Retirement Plan was funded every year for the next twenty years with $300,000.00. In twenty years, there should be a corpus of $6,000,000.00.

Without question, it might not make sense for the W-2 employee to fund the maximum of $300,000.00 into a charitable retirement plan, but it clearly demonstrates how this type of planning "blows the doors off" traditional or secular financial planning. Which of the above plans, both managed by the same financial planner, using the same investment models, will provide you the greatest annual income tax benefits and superior retirement lifestyle?

Charitable Retirement Planning is a bet you will live. Most life insurance is a bet you will die. I am betting and planning on both. Thanks to Schedule A, Line 19, my wife and I will retire in style.

Remember, everything in the tax code has some form of cap or limitation on contributions. If your plan is to live and enjoy retirement, you need to find better tools than qualified plans to retire in style. Now that I have your attention, this book will introduce you to many other overlooked tax planning strategies.

Hands down, if you want to reduce your income tax and retire in style, read this book.

Chapter 2
Rich verses Wealthy

Have you heard this statement?

Rich people are good at making money. Wealthy people are good at making money and keeping more of it!

Many people wrongly assume the reasons they are not making money is due to the investment rate of return or bad timing of the market or global economic issues. None of that matters. Until you understand how to control tax triggers and tax erosion, you might become rich by accident. Let me prove to you why and how you must avoid tax triggers and erosion.

It is not an issue of your investments but avoiding two critical wealth building mistakes. Wealthy people understand how to avoid tax triggers and control the erosion of wealth from cascading taxes.

Mistake #1. Tax Triggers.
These are wages or investment monies gained or wealth transfers which trigger Income Tax, Capital Gains Tax and / or Estate Taxes.

Learning "HOW" to minimize or eliminate your tax trigger(s) is a concept of learning the difference between Ownership verses Control. From your beginning, you have been trained to be a taxpayer and an owner. Chances are, your paid advisors are teaching you the same concept. Except for some wages, all Capital Gains Taxes and Estate Taxes are optional - provided you use structures and strategies to avoid triggering those tax events prior to the sale or asset transfer.

Therefore, when making an investment the most important question is not what risk will I incur if there is a downside turn, but rather the right question should be, what is my Zero Tax Exit strategy when I sell because it was a successful investment? I am hopeful your due diligence will steer you away from poor investments and yes, the IRS does reward you with a small token benefit (capital loss carry forward) for being a good loser.

When you watch television or read magazines about financial advisors lauding how great their investments preformed and how they had little or no tax on the growth, it is because they have learned how to control those tax triggers in a tax-exempt structure. There are several structures which provide tax free growth. I call these Tax Friendly environments. Finding the right one, two or three for you is the beginning of your wealth journey.

Mistake #2. Tax Erosion.
Erosion is the wealth lost from the overpayment of a tax that could have remained under your control to produce more money for you and your family.

For example; if you overpaid a tax this year by $100,000.00, what did you really lose? First, your balance sheet is $100,000.00 less for life. Next, the growth on that $100,000.00 is lost for life. (Many advisors call that Lost Opportunity) For Example, if the growth would have been five percent per year for the next twenty years, your lost opportunity is not the $100,000.00 of growth. Assuming a net five percent return, it is the compounding annual growth ($5,000.00) each year over the next twenty years that will cost your estate over $171,264.03 of total interest on that lost $100,000.00.

And finally, if those funds are growing in a Tax Hostile environment versus a Tax Friendly environment, the differences are enormous.

What if (theoretically) you had an investment opportunity which doubled annually for the next 21 years? You place the investment in a tax hostile environment with a state and federal tax rate of 40%. You fund $1.00 into the investment. At the end of year one, you have $2.00 minus 40% tax on the dollar earned, which is now $1.60 to be reinvested. That $1.60 doubles the next year to $3.20 minus 40% tax on the new $1.60, which continues forward. That tax erosion cascades over the next 21 years and you end up with less than $13,000 of after tax money.

But what if it could grow both tax trigger and tax erosion free?

Imagine... What if you had the same investment opportunity above that grew 100% per year in a tax friendly environment? Let's fund $1.00 in your tax-exempt investment vehicle – which is a tax friendly environment. At the end of year one, you will have $2.00 and no tax erosion. Year two, $4.00 and no tax erosion. Year three, $8.00 and so on. At the end of twenty-one year's your investment would have grown to nearly $1,050,000.00 - never subjected to any tax.

The next logical question is this. Since you used a tax-exempt vehicle to grow this money free of tax erosion and tax triggers, how do you get it out? Back to basics, since we made a decision to start the investment in the first place, that means we also figured out our tax efficient exit. Remember, always know what your tax exit options are before you invest.

This is another principle of how and why charitable retirement planning vehicles helps you reduce your income tax and increase your retirement income. Failing to incorporate Schedule A, Line 19 into your plan means you will over pay your income tax this year and fail to retire in style!

Chapter 3
Ownership vs. Control

Consider this. If you control an asset and you reap all the same benefits as if you owned the asset, and you realized some form of tax or wealth benefits, does it make sense to actually own the asset?

Rich people do not embrace this idea, but wealthy people do. Here are a few points to ponder. If you both own and control the asset (risk), its growth is subject to every layer of taxation and you have no level of asset protection in case of a law suit.

Maximum Wealth Control is the balance of both asset protection and tax efficiency. Simply stated, if you lose the asset in a law suit, you no longer have a tax dilemma.

There are many structures and entities to provide you some form of asset protection. For many business owners these include properly formed and administered Corporation, Limited Liability Companies or Limited Partnership. With qualified legal counsel, each of these entities can provide you a major degree of asset protection in which to operate an active trade or business.

For investors not operating as a trade or business, the Limited Liability Company, Limited Partnership or even a Corporation acting as a Holding Company can bring a strong degree of asset protection. For the more sophisticated taxpayer, seeking a higher degree of asset protection, you may want to seek advance planning tools such as a Delaware Incomplete Non-Grantor (DING) Trust, Nevada Incomplete-gift Non-Grantor (NING) Trust or a Domestic Asset Protection Trust (DAPT). In addition to these, the new Private Retirement Trust (PRT) in California is gaining noticeable effectiveness.

All the above are beautiful, time tested asset protection vehicles that can provide you a high degree of safety and security when drafted by a qualified professional and properly funded. When lay persons try to save a few bucks by doing it themselves or copying documents off the Internet, the results are overwhelmingly disastrous.

There are several issues to address when seeking asset protection. First, you need to learn a word called Fraudulent Conveyance. There are two types of fraudulent transfer(s)—*actual fraud* and *constructive fraud*. Simply, if you attempt to avoid a debt by transferring or gifting money to another party or company, you may become subject to a civil action. The creditor has been damaged because of your transfer or default. Case law and the doctrine of Fraudulent Conveyance date back to 1601, the Twyne's Case in the United Kingdom.

Why is understanding Fraudulent Conveyance important if our only objective is to create a degree of asset protection? Depending on your state, the amount of your personal estate that you place into an asset protection structure may have a limit. For example, in California, most courts will deem it permissible and not a fraudulent conveyance, if you transfer approximately thirty five percent or less of your assets into an asset protection vehicle. Which means, to avoid triggering a possible Fraudulent Conveyance ruling down the road, you cannot put all your eggs into one basket!

Finding the balance, determining which assets of your estate and what will be the tax consequences of using an asset protection vehicle requires a multi-faceted approach to successfully employ a defendable strategy.

There is a fine line by creating some level of asset protection for part of your estate. I will be the first to advocate asset protection must be done with qualified and experienced attorneys. On countless occasions I am asked to review a document off the Internet or from some on-line legal document company. Failure to customize these powerful asset protection tools to you, the asset and your state law can and will have a detrimental impact. If you have or will have something of value, spend the money on an attorney and protect it. Once protected, then figure out how to solve the tax problem.

Chapter 4
The Four Phases of Money

At some point, you will either begin work as an adult, hit the lottery or become the beneficiary of an estate. Chances are, you will start life as an employee. This begins the Four Phases of Money.

Creation

Accumulation

Utilization

Distribution

At this point, you are creating your riches. You earn money for the services you provide, you are paid a wage or salary, minus hefty deductions many of which you do not understand, and then you deposit your net earnings into a bank account. If you deposit more than you spend, you are now accumulating riches.

If you spent more than you earned, this is the wrong book for you. Try the credit repair or bankruptcy section of the library.

Now that you are accumulating riches, you put that money to work. The goal should be for your money to make money for you. Hopefully with the highest degree of asset protection and least tax exposure.

You continue to work, creating and accumulating more money over time with the objective being some form of financial independence – which is different for everyone. As you enter those retirement years, the creation model tapers off. Now you are dependent on the accumulation phase being large enough to provide you income to support your Utilization Phase (retirement).

Thanks to your savings and investments, you enjoy retirement as you ride into the sunset to that final day. Upon your death(s), your estate will pass to your heirs. This is called the Distribution Phase. Your estate may be divided into three categories. Part to your heirs, part to the government in the form of taxes and part to charity.

The part to heirs and charity are self-explanatory. Most of Americans are completely unaware that certain assets they own will not receive a Step Up In Basis adjustment upon their death(s). The Step Up In Basis rule adjusts the basis (amount you purchased it for) to the current fair market value – tax free. For example, your home or personally owned stocks. Simply, all that prior appreciation is no longer a tax event for your heirs when they liquidate those assets. Conversely, had you sold an appreciated asset prior to your death, the appreciation would have been taxed.

The Step Up In Basis Rule is another Best Kept Tax Secret. However, to use it, your cost is high. You are dead. And yes, it is a one-time use, per person tax strategy.

Here is what you may not know. Income in Respect to a Decedent (IRD) Tax. These are monies due to the decedent and will pass to the heir or estate. Such as, IRA Distributions, retirement plan assets, unpaid interest and dividends, salary, wages, and commissions, plus others.

These post mortem taxable assets when transferred to natural beings or certain trusts will be subjected to tax. As such, you need to understand what the tax treatment will be upon your death.

The most common mistake I see is the following. Husband and Wife build an estate. They prudently handle their financial affairs. They have a financial planner, insurance agent, banker, accountant and attorney. Their estate is $2,000,000.00. Therefore, no estate tax issue to complicate this example.

Husband dies first, then wife. Their revocable trust states everything goes equally to their heirs, minus a ten percent gift to their church. On the surface this seems like an excellent plan.

The planning mistake missed by ALL their advisors was the Traditional IRA valued at $200,000.00. Let's do the math. The remainder of the personal estate is valued at $1,800,000.00 which consist of the house, checking and savings, life insurance policies and tangible personal assets. Since their trust mandates ten percent goes to charity, the trust will gift $180,000.00 of the $1.8M to charity – per their instructions.

Depending on the IRA beneficiary form and state law, all the IRA or at the minimum, all of the IRA will go to their heirs – subject to IRD tax. In other words, added to their income. More in IRA distributions later.

A better design solution would have been for the clients to designate their church as the death beneficiary of their IRA. Since the church is a tax-exempt entity, there would be no tax event, which means a full benefit of $200,000.00 for the church. Saving $50,000.00 or more of income tax!

This also means instead of their heirs having to pay tax on the IRA proceeds, they actually inherit more because now their inheritance, the $1.8M, which received a full step up in basis, creates zero tax.

Proper planning would have put $1.8M tax free to the heirs, $200,000.00 to charity and ZERO to the IRS.

Tip. You must direct and authorize your advisors to collaborate on your overall plan to avoid simple tax planning mistakes like this one. You would be amazed how often this mistake is made every day.

Chapter 5
Maximum Wealth Control – Tax Free Sale of Business or Appreciated Assets

Your primary objective for wealth creation, accumulation, utilization and distribution should have four primary vehicles to reduce, and in many cases, eliminate the bulk of your lifetime tax burdens.

These vehicles include the use of a business entity such as a Limited Liability Company or Limited Partnership, an Insurance product possibly structured in an Insurance Trust, a charitable vehicle and a Defective or Dynasty Trust. Depending on your asset base and objectives, a structure using the tools above will provide you Maximum Wealth Control.

First, you need to accept the fact that you, and the bulk of life insurance agents and financial planners, do not know how to properly use life insurance for life planning. Most agents sell you products designed to address risk due to your businesses, or if you become incapacitated or die at an early age. The primary benefit of the life product is to provide tax free funds to the beneficiaries. We love that part, but again, you had to die to make that type of product fulfill its purpose. But what if there was a way to use life insurance to create zero tax income for you? And no, I do not mean borrowing against your cash value build up in the policy.

Ask yourself this question. Why do billionaires buy and own large quantities of paid up, whole and universal life products? Is it because they need life insurance? That answer is a definite no. They do not need life insurance, but they love life insurance because of how they can use it while they are breathing. Remember, they use the same tax code as you to control their tax liability. Sadly, your insurance agent probably does not know why billionaires use life insurance daily in their wealth plans to make money. If they do know how to do it, great, now is the time for your advisors to share with you how you can do what the billionaires are doing!

Life Insurance can be purchased with a guaranteed death benefit. By the way, the bulk of life policies do not have a "guaranteed" death benefit.

The difference is enormous. The key difference is the death benefit can be used as collateral for a loan. For example; What if you had a $5,000,000.00 guaranteed death benefit? What if you decided to use the guaranteed death benefit as collateral for a bona fide loan each year? Let's start putting pieces together.

What is a bona fide loan? It must have three components in order for the loan to be considered bona fide or verified. It must have collateral, a payment plan and a fair interest rate. We addressed the collateral part using life insurance (or other assets such as real estate), the payment plan is selected according to the period you desire, and the interest rate simply needs to be something slightly higher than the mid-term Applicable Federal Rate (AFR. See IRS Section 1274d).

Here is where things get a little complex. What if you were going to sell a $5,000,000.00 parcel of highly appreciated real estate or business? Let's assume the basis is zero which means the transaction would be subject to multiple layers of tax. Federal Long-Term Capital Gains, some states treat the sale as ordinary income or they have a capital gains tax, possible Net Income Investment Tax (NET), possible recapture tax due to prior deprecation, and the list continues to grow dependent upon the nature and character of the asset.

Let's use thirty percent as a very generous, low tax rate. This means that if you do nothing to address the future tax trigger, you will give approximately $1,500,000.00 of real money to the taxing authorities, and you will take home $3,500,000.00 of after tax money to reinvest into new taxable investments. From a prior chapter, we discussed the importance of doing some level of asset protection to safe guard the funds with a degree of asset protection.

Side note. Most people selling highly appreciated real property assets are taught one strategy to defer the tax bill using a 1031 exchange. While I do like that strategy for those growing their wealth, as long as they are not currently or will not shortly become subject to estate taxes, I often recommend the use of that tool. However, if you are, or will shortly become subject to estate taxes, this tool goes way down on my list of effective ways to defer or sell assets tax smart. Again, these are great tools for wealth creation and accumulation up to the estate tax limit which for 2017 was $5,600,000.00, then doubled to $11,200,000.00 per person under the Tax Cuts and Jobs Act of 2018. However, that new permanent tax provision reverts in 2027 back to the prior code. Simply stated, the estate tax roller coaster is open for business. Be careful gifting assets as great care must be considered since the Step Up In Basis rule was preserved in this tax reform.

With no planning, you lost $1.5M. Not only did you lose $1.5M on the transaction, the lost opportunity on that money for life is huge! How do billionaires solve this problem?

Remember, the four primary vehicles from the beginning of this chapter? Let's put them together. Since you are going to make a $1.5M donation to your least favorite charities, the Federal and State taxing authorities (charities), why not capture some charitable tax planning benefits to control this wealth loss? There are several powerful ways to integrate a charitable vehicle into this model to reduce or zero out the tax.

One simple model may be to combine a part sale and part blended gift structure using a FLiP Charitable Remainder Uni-Trust (CRUT). You could gift a determined percentage of the real estate into the CRUT. If the percentage is calculated properly, that means the portion gifted into the CRUT will bypass all tax exposures upon sale and the portion you retained in your name will be taxable. The balance is then the charitable income tax deduction you are entitled to use on your 1040, Schedule A, Line 19. In other words, you sold tax free, the funds in the CRUT can be reinvested into prudent type investments, and you can determine when you would like to start receiving income from the CRUT.

Timing is HUGE when doing any level of charitable tax planning, especially when the sale of stocks, land or businesses are involved. BEFORE you sign ANY listing agreement, shake hands with a buyer, execute or accept a purchase letter of intent, etc., you should meet with legal and tax counsel to discuss the procedures and timing to use a charitable tax strategy to reduce or eliminate a tax event. In other words, do the planning first, then begin the sale process.

The court case you will need to look at is Ferguson vs. Commissioner, No. 98-70095, 9th Circuit, decided April 07, 1999. By failing to consult with your tax advisors in advance of a preparatory sale event, you could end up closing all productive tax reduction and elimination strategies.

By incorporating the proper charitable tax planning tool prior to "beginning the process of selling an appreciated event" will most likely reduce or zero out the tax upon the sale event and provide you greater income for life. Tip. Duplicate what the billionaires do when they sell highly appreciated assets. You have access to the same tax code, but you may not have advisors who know how to do this.

Chapter 6
Research and Development Tax Credits

Business owners and entrepreneurs often overlook this powerful tax strategy and assume they must have large, multi-million-dollar on-site laboratories or breakthrough research data to claim the credits. Others fear they'll face complex tax calculations or **trigger an IRS audit**. But small and midsize businesses that employ engineers or outsource product testing can claim R&D credits. These credits have become more attractive for small companies in recent years because they've been simplified, can be transferred in an acquisition, and can be taken retroactively. And, they are particularly good for startups, since R&D costs incurred in years when a company has no income can be carried forward to offset taxes on future profits up to 20 years.

Birth of the R&D Tax Credit

With widespread concern that the U.S. economic performance had fallen well below its potential, Congress passed "The Economic Recovery Tax Act (ERTA) of 1981. The ERTA was intended to act as an economic stimulus that would encourage investment within the United States under Internal Revenue Code Section 41 known as the Research and Experimentation Tax Credit or the R&D Tax Credit.

Does the U.S. Need this R&D Tax Credit?

The Credit was tailored to reverse the decline in U.S. research spending by providing an incentive that was premised on benefitting increases in (as opposed to total) year over year research spending. Globally, the United States ranks in eightieth position as favorable countries to perform R&D.

Why has my CPA not pursued this Credit for Me?

Tax consultants estimate that eligible businesses obtain as little as five percent of the main domestic tax breaks that they are entitled to claim. That means firms are leaving tens of billions of dollars on the table every year. Out of 1.78 million corporate tax returns in the U.S., only about 20,000 claimed any of the three-dozen main business tax credits in the code, according to IRS estimates. Small or solo practice CPA firms simply do not have the time or staff needed to be proficient in every part of the code.

For most accounting practitioners, it is an issue of acquiring knowledge and systems for the benefit of all their clients—not specialty planning like R&D for one or two of their client base. As you read more about this strategy and determine you may become eligible, or if your current tax advisor does not have a few years of prior experience, now is not to time to experiment on you. Ask your trusted tax advisor to bring in experienced advisors to determine if you are eligible and if yes, what amount of tax credit might you qualify to receive?

Caution: The key words in the paragraph above was trusted and experienced. Great care must be exercised here as there are planners who present themselves as R&D experts, who are not attorneys, accountants, or have any form of license whatsoever. Some of these advisors do great work; some take advantage of you. Therefore, you need your trusted CPA involved in this process. Some of these promoters promise huge tax credits for you. The issue here is not the quality of the work but addressing the most important question first. If you do qualify for the credit, can you use it? I have seen several business owners spend several hundred thousand dollars on these promoters, simply to end up with a pile of pretty paper and tons of documentation for a credit that does not provide you a current or near current tax benefit. Something this complex requires the integration of your advisors working as a team. I love R&D Tax Credits, but only when it makes sense!

What is the Four-Part Test? Here is the short version of the tax code.

Generally, qualified research is an activity or project undertaken by a taxpayer (directly or through direct funding of a third party on the taxpayer's behalf) that comprises each of the four distinct elements:

- Permitted Purpose: The purpose of the activity or project must be to create new (or improve existing) functionality, performance, reliability, or quality of a business component.

- Elimination of Uncertainty: The taxpayer must intend to discover information that would eliminate uncertainty concerning the development or improvement of the business component.

- Process of Experimentation: The taxpayer must undergo a systematic process designed to evaluate one or more alternatives to achieve a result where the capability or the method of achieving that result, or the appropriate design of that result, is uncertain as of the beginning of the taxpayer's research activities.

- Technological in Nature: The process of experimentation used to discover information must fundamentally rely on principles of the physical or biological sciences, engineering, or computer science.

What Type of Industries Qualify?

- Automobile parts manufacturing

- Tool and Die making

- Aerospace parts manufacturing

- Design/Build contracting

- Structural engineering

- Medical equipment manufacturing

- Civil and Environmental engineering

- Illumination engineering

- Biomedical engineering

- Architectural design / CAD

- Computer modeling / Software / App dev.

- Examples of Activities that may qualify:

- Testing of new concepts

- Developing or testing of new products/materials

- Paying outside consultants/contractors to perform any of these activities

- Development of new or enhanced formulations

- Improving existing products

- Trial and error experimentation

- Developing or improving production or manufacturing processes

- Design and analysis of prototypes or models

- Developing, implementing or upgrading systems/software

I have seen this tax credit save businesses from bankruptcy, increase net profit margins, inspire creation of new products, new jobs, growth and expansion, not to forget building the value of the business – which directly impacts the value upon the sale of the business. Yes, there is an economic breakeven point for the small business conducting limited amounts of qualified R&D work. Regardless, you need to determine if you would benefit.

Also, this credit can be used for work completed retroactively during the past three years under the Federal Tax Code, and up to four years under some State Tax Codes. For example, two years ago your company invented a new widget. You spent $2,000,000.00 designing, testing and developing the widget which does meet the criteria to qualify for the R&D credit. Last year, the new revenue from that product has created a large income tax burden. The new revenue is continuing to produce increased sales revenue and your tax bill is skyrocketing. Now is the time to discuss if that work qualifies for R&D Credit and restating and amending those prior returns. If you fail to quantify the R&D work and restate those returns timely, you will miss the window to claim those tax credits! Remember, tax credits are dollar for dollar.

Practice Tip. If you do restate and amend prior returns, which means you may qualify to receive a generous refund, it would be wise to plan on an audit. Here is where the experience of the R&D practitioner pays off. That experienced advisor will expect an audit for restating prior returns. He or she can greatly control the outcome of the potential audit by not being greedy with the numbers. A phrase one of my favorite R&D CPAs uses is "Pigs get fat, hogs get slaughtered". He has never lost an R&D audit and has rescued millions of overpaid tax dollars for his clients!

Rip off tip. Be careful of R&D Tax experts who preform analysis using an engagement fee based upon the amount of tax credit they determine you might be eligible to receive. For example, if the R&D analysis indicate you are entitled to a $5M tax credit, they will seek to be paid based upon a percentage of that analysis.

The real question here is can you use a tax credit? What if you have a pile of net operating losses? What if you have very limited income tax exposure in the first place? In other words, you paid a huge fee to create a tax credit that may provide you little if any actual financial benefit. Don't get me wrong, there are many who qualify and need to utilize this benefit. Sadly, there are many businesses that qualify, but cannot apply the benefit to their tax return now or in years to come.

Next, ask if the R&D advisor will provide audit protection services at no cost to you. When done properly, most will guarantee their work. This does not mean they will pay any tax or penalty, but their representation of the audit is done at their expense.

Chapter 7
Export Tax Benefits / IC-DISC

Are you exporting US Produced Products or Delivering Services Overseas?

Since 1971, many business owners who export products or services outside of the United States are missing out on a generous federal income tax reduction strategy. This strategy did not become popular until the Jobs and Growth Tax Relief Reconciliation Act of 2003 which lowered the capital gains tax rate making it much more attractive for exporters. With the recent passage of the American Taxpayer Relief Act of 2012, this strategy has permanence in the tax code.

The strategy is called an IC-DISC. It is an acronym for Interest Charge – Domestic International Sales Corporation (IC-DISC). The IC-DISC is a separate legal entity and Corporations, individuals and partnerships are eligible to receive the tremendous Federal income tax savings available under the Internal Revenue Code. You can find the complex regulations under Internal Revenue Code Sections 991-997 for US taxpayers and it is NOT considered a tax shelter. Each state taxing authority will determine if they will or will not conform to the Federal Code. For example, California does not.

If your business has an annual tax liability of more than $100,000 a year and provides services or manufactures products in the following fields which are distributed and used abroad, you may be eligible:

- Agriculture Grown in the US

- Software Development

- Food Processing

- Medical Devices

- Pharmaceutical

- Metal Fabrication

- Manufacturing

- Recycling of Scrap Metal or Paper

- Distribution

This is an executive summary of how it works. The exporting company (using experienced legal and tax counsel) creates a new entity and elects Federal non-taxable IC-DISC status. The US exporter pays a deductible commission to IC-DISC (39.6% Federal tax deductions 2017 tax rate). The income accumulates untaxed in the IC-DISC. The IC-DISC pays a qualified dividend to its shareholders at a lower tax rate, typically twenty to twenty three percent. Simplified, this is a tax savings of approximately twenty percent.

Additional benefits include:

Permanent Federal tax law

Flexibility to use the plan based on two different sales ratios

Increased liquidity for the shareholders or business

Ability to leverage cost of capital

Make dividends paid by C Corp tax deductible

Various succession planning opportunities

No prohibition when claiming Domestic Production

Activities Deduction (DPAD).

If your company is transacting business outside of the United States, uses overseas distribution or crosses any border (including software downloads), this strategy may greatly benefit you and your company. Another "cool" tax secret.

Chapter 8
Cost Segregation Study

Cost Segregation is a process of identifying personal property real estate (commercial or residential) and separating the personal assets for federal tax and accounting benefits. Simply stated, this process reclassifies personal property and allows you the ability to shorten the deprecation time to increase your income tax savings. These may include certain construction costs, exterior property improvements, and non-structural building components. Instead of using the standard 27.5 and 39-year depreciation calculations, certain aspects of the property may be depreciated over a lessor time cycle such as five, seven or fifteen-year periods.

If you purchased, remodeled, expanded or constructed a building after 1987, you may have an eligible asset that may qualify for cost segregation. If those expenses were greater than $750,000.00, you may need a formal engineering study for commercial type assets or residential assets with a basis of $150,000.00. The process and study may also uncover retroactive tax benefits for older properties as well.

Aside from the obvious objective to reduce your tax bill, there are several other benefits to consider.

1. By applying the tax benefits from the study, it frees up cash to allow you to address current business or capital development.

2. Proactive planning provides you strong defense in the event of an audit. Failure to properly document asset classifications and the associated costs can result in time and money wasted on a lengthy audit. Remember, pigs get fat, hogs get slaughtered.

3. Another powerful play is the retroactive cost segregation analysis on older assets. In prior tax code, the rules allowed you a four-year catch-up period. Many began using this strategy in 1996 when the code was modified. However, cost segregation has been around since 1987. It is worth the discussion with your CPA to explore if this strategy will benefit you.

4. You might realize some estate tax benefits. (Death Tax for Successful People)

5. Under Code Section 481(a), a post mortem estate tax benefit may be possible by applying a cost segregation study for the decedent's estate for a possible pre-stepped up tax basis. Be aware, this play may need to be executed prior to the decedents final income tax return being filed.

Pain Points. This is not for everyone. Before you meet with your tax advisor, get smart about the terms, the law and yourself. Do you plan to sell one or more of the assets in question within the next 3 years? Do you plan to do any major remodel or expansion? What is the likelihood for the asset being vacant due to external economic conditions? Questions like these being addressed in advance of the meeting are extremely helpful and will provide value to your tax advisor.

If the initial analysis indicates a positive value, after factoring in the cost of the study, depreciation recapture and not being too aggressive with your deduction (possible audit), you may find this powerful secret a hidden gem to help reduce your income tax liability.

Business and property owners need to consider the following. At some point, this asset will change hands, either by divorce, law suit, sale or death. You should always be ready to sell the asset. My question is this. Do you have a strategy to sell the asset zero tax when that date arrives? Most are shocked at the tax rates and most advisors do not have tools to help you address this tax burden. Thankfully, you have a copy of this book and the answer to that zero-tax sale event is in here.

Chapter 9
1031 Exchanges Are Tax Bombs for the Wealthy!

Almost everyone has heard of a 1031 exchange strategy. That is no secret. Simply, think of this as a property swap with no immediate tax consequences by deferring gain. The first tax-deferred like-kind exchange was not included in our first income tax code adopted by Congress in 1918. Shortly thereafter, in 1921, Congress created Section 202(c) of the Internal Code allowing investors to exchange securities and non-like-kind properties. The Revenue Act of 1924 quickly eliminated the non-like-kind property provisions. Later in 1928, section 112(b) was amended to be tax-deferred like-kind exchanges. Finally, in 1935, we see the introduction of an exchange using a Qualified Intermediary and the "cash in lieu of" clause was upheld.

In 1954, the Federal Tax Code changed Section 112(b)(1) number to Section 1031 of the Internal Revenue Code which laid down the ground work of our current day like-kind exchange program. I share this to help you understand there is a huge body of law behind the 1031 Exchange process. Which also means, there are piles of tax court cases to rely upon when or if an exchange violates proven tax code.

The 1031 Exchange is an exemption and allows you to postpone paying tax on the current gain (trigger event) if your goal is to reinvest the proceeds into a similar property. This is an excellent tax deferral strategy for those who are not subject to estate tax. Since none of us know when we are going to die, if you have an estate that exceeds the Life Time Unified Credit (the estate tax exemption for 2017 was $5.49M per person - double for 2018), although your estate will get a Step Up in Basis adjustment, the value will be reported on your death tax return 706.

Granted, the Step Up in Basis rule is great, but you had to die to use it. Pretty expensive strategy and it is a one-time use for the bulk of us. If you do multiple 1031 exchanges to create your wealth, if your estate does not exceed the Life Time Unified Credit, the 1031 strategy paid off well to your family.

Upon your death, your real property assets Step Up In Basis and the estate transfers with little, if any tax, to your heirs. Yeah! However, if the estate exceeded your Life Time Credit, your heirs will not inherit the full value of your estate.

Here is the tax bomb! If you used the 1031 concept to create your wealth beyond the Life Time Unified Credit, you have converted a portion of your deferred taxable estate, which will get a Step Up In Basis upon your death, it has become an estate tax liability. In other words, once your estate is larger than the Life Time Unified Credit, you should consider using some other tax planning strategy to create and accumulate more wealth.

Don't get me wrong. I love the 1031 concept to create and accumulate wealth up to your unified credit. Key here is to get out of that rut once you cross that tax threshold. At that point, you need to graduate up to higher levels of tax planning and wealth building efficiency. Sadly, this is where you will discover the limitation of your advisors' tax knowledge and the reason many of you purchased this book.

Once your wealth exceeds the Life Time Unified Credit, you must learn the difference between Ownership vs Control. Ask any billionaire to choose only one of the two, they will always elect control. Ownership is taxable, and subject to creditors and predators. As you graduate to higher levels of wealth and tax knowledge efficiency, you will probably find the need to graduate up to higher level advisors.

Chapter 10
Finding Strong Advisors

No advisor knows everything. Considering the multitude of investment opportunities, your short and long-term goals, our ever-changing tax and probate codes, it is impossible for anyone to stay abreast of everything. But one commonality I find prevalent among consumers and advisors is the failure to collaborate.

By definition, to collaborate means working together to produce or create something. I am often asked by clients to define what I mean by this statement. If you have a proactive team of advisors, they will be happy to meet with you. In fact, some advisors in the financial services industry are required to communicate with you on a periodic basis. That is not an example of collaboration but a perfect example of the industry trying to cover their butt from law suits.

Here is your first question to determine if you have individual or collaborative advisors.

When was the last time your accountant, attorney, financial advisor and insurance agent were all in the same room or at least a conference call at the same time discussing you? Maybe one out of one hundred reading this book can answer with a positive response. Here are what consumers tell me. Ed, my accountant said to do this. My attorney said not to do that. My financial advisor said to do something else. My banker said to do nothing. Who can I trust to help me?

First, you may be the one to blame for your advisors not knowing how to help you. Chances are, you picked individual advisors to address a need or immediate problem. For example, you opened an IRA account. You needed a Will or Trust. You needed to form a business entity. You needed life insurance. You needed a loan. Separately, these are normal, important parts of a person planning to survive in today's complex world. Chances are, you do not have a coordinated plan.

Second, have you identified and written out your short term and long-term objectives? If yes, do "all" of your advisor have a copy of your objectives? Next, how often do you update your objectives?

Without a plan, here are the standard questions you will hear from reactive advisors. Do you have a trust? Do you have enough insurance? What interest are your paying on your mortgage? When do you want to retire and what income do you feel you will need to live on when you retire?

Please wake me up when these boring, reactive questions are completed. And by the way, you do not need to have a team meeting for those levels of questions because those are the wrong questions.

What if your objectives were better defined with:

- I desire a lifestyle that includes....
- I desire a retirement lifestyle that includes...
- Show me how to define the social, emotional and spiritual aspects of my life in order for my family to do the most good for ourselves and our country.
- Show me how to find happiness in everything I do.
- Show me how to avoid spoiling my children.

In order to obtain those goals...

- Show me how to reduce my income tax for life by thirty to sixty percent annually.
- Show me how to grow my wealth free of capital gains tax.
- Show me how to sell assets capital gains tax free.
- Show me how to create zero tax income for my retirement years.
- Show me how to sell my business with minimal or no tax.
- Show me how to transfer my wealth to my heir's estate tax free.

Depending on your wealth and activity, at least once a year you need to direct some level of collaboration between your advisors. Your tax advisor will be a key player. If you are a business owner, you may need to do this type of meeting more than once a year. But if your activity warrants one meeting per year, I suggest a meeting after September 15 but before December 1.

During that time period, your team should be able to provide enough data about your spending and investments to predict your end of year tax numbers. At that point, your team, using your defined objectives, should be able to provide you solutions to address your end of year tax report card. Armed with hard data, you can implement strategies to reduce your tax. Remember, rich people are good at making money, wealthy people are good at making money and keeping more of it! Your Form 1040 is both a report of you and how effective your group of advisors played the tax game this year.

Every year, I get multiple phone calls the last week of December begging for that magic solution to solve a painful tax event. Remember this. Procrastinators over pay their tax. Waiting until the last minute robs you of proactive advice and many planning opportunities that could have increased your bottom line. Also, when you elect to over pay your tax, it was both a current wealth loss multiplied by the lost opportunity on the money it could have earned for you and your family for years to come. Let that sink in for a minute. For example. If you overpaid your income or capital gains tax by $10,000.00 this year, you lost the $10,000.00 and all the growth that $10,000.00 could have produced for you for the remainder of your life. When you think of it like that, how much did you really lose?

Proactive "end of year" tax and wealth planning will make you money. Since your advisors do not know how to do collaborative planning, it will be up to you to lead the pack. They want to do collaborative planning, they have heard of the concept, but few know how to do it or start the process.

Remember, you picked these individual advisors. It will be up to you to turn them into a team!

Chapter 11
Charitable Tax Planning Basics

This section will help you begin your journey of understanding the rules and parameters of using Schedule A, Line 19 to your benefit. This chapter is probably the most powerful and best kept tax secret! Let's begin with some basics.

Deductions for charitable giving can be claimed on IRS Form 1040, not 1040A or 1040EZ. In the world of tax, we call that the long form. Remember, you are not required to claim any deductions or expenses each year. You have the right to pay full rate, that is, claim no deductions. I had a meeting this past year where a person was complaining about how thick his tax return was and what it costs to prepare the return. I promptly informed him he had the right to bypass all that CPA preparation cost and formality and pay the maximum rate. And yes, he gave me that have you lost your mind look!

The charitable tax code has a hierarchy of order and deductibility for gifts with cash considered as a priority over stock or real estate. This is the very simplified version for 2017.

1. Cash gifts to 50% AGI limit. Improved to 60% for 2018!

2. Appreciated gifts elected to be deducted at cost basis to 50% limit.

3. Unrelated use tangible personal property deducted at cost basis to 50% limit.

4. Short-term capital gain deducted at cost basis to 50% limit.

5. Appreciated stock or land deducted at fair market value to 30% limit.

6. Gifts "for the use of" a charity deducted to 30% limit.

7. Cash to private foundation deducted at 30% limit.

8. Public stock to private foundation deducted at fair market value to 20% limit.

9. Land or private stock to private foundation at cost basis to 20% limit.

10. Carry forwards of 50% limit gifts.

11. Carry forwards of 30% limit cash gifts to private foundations.

12. Carry forwards of 30% appreciated property gifts to public foundations.

13. Carry forwards of 20% limit gifts to private foundations.

At this point, you may be wondering the difference of public and private foundations, why their limits and variations are on carry forward rules, etc. Simply, it is a matter of how the federal tax code has matured over the decades. The bulk of this is based on millions of gifts or transactions, tested since 1917.

Most charities you support are public charities. These are statutory public charities, public charities supported through donations, public charities receiving exempt function income or supporting organizations. You and I see these operating as churches, community foundations, major charities like the Red Cross and Salvation Army. These organizations are primarily supported by the public and these organizations are subject to more public scrutiny which helps the organization better comply with all regulatory rules. They are very transparent.

There are several types of private foundation structures. These may be independent foundations, family foundations, corporate foundations, international foundations or private operating foundations. These structures normally have minimal donors. These tend to have more stringent operating rules and regulations than public charities. There are many prohibitions of donor self-dealing, limits on the amount of stock they can donate, and many more issues.

Here are some code references to better understand the various technical differences.

- Self-Dealing Taxes – CFR 26.53 Sec. 4941(d)(1) and 4941(c)(2)

- Tax on Failure to Distribute Income – Sec. 4942(g)(1)(A)

- Tax on Excess Business Holdings – Sec. 4943

- Tax on Jeopardizing Investments – Sec. 4944(c)

- Tax on Taxable Expenditures – 4945(h)

- Private Foundation Net Investment Income Excise Tax - 4940(e)

- Charitable Organization Tax Shelter Disclosure

To add more confusion, it is possible for an organization to operate as a not for profit such as your local hospital. The hospital itself does not have an equity owner per se, it operates as a public benefit foundation. Most hospitals will also have a charitable fund-raising arm to support the objectives of the hospital. Hence, you may be approached to donate to the hospital, but in fact, you are donating to the foundation (charity) that supports the hospital. You could technically donate to the not for profit, but since it does not have a charitable exemption under code section 501(c)(3), you would not get a charitable income tax deduction.

Also, charities are required to provide you a written receipt for gifts more than $250.00. That is another indicator your gift is to a charitable organization recognized under IRS Publication 78.

Let's put this data to work. Assume your CPA has completed your draft return for this year prior to December 31. Your CPA explains your Taxable Adjusted Gross Income (TAGI) will be $100,000.00. Your CPA shows you the Federal and State tax rates. At that point, if you elect to do nothing else this tax year that will be your tax bill.

But here you sit, looking at that tax bill wondering what else can you do at this point? If you have discretionary money or a portfolio of appreciated assets such as stock or real estate, now is the time to have a discussion about Scheduled A, Line 19.

For example. You have a block of stock you purchased for $10,000.00 ten years ago. The stock did very well the first seven years, but it plateaued. In fact, the line is flat, and all indications are it is about to go south. The current value of the stock is $60,000.00. If you sell, you will have a long-term capital gain and some states may tax the gain as ordinary income like California. There may be additional taxes such as the Net Investment Tax, often referred to as Obama Tax or a future replacement tax. Many will have their hand out to participate in your financial success, unless you control this trigger event.

If you decide to use part or all that stock to fund some form of a charitable retirement plan, the gift to the charity will fall under the hierarchy sentence numbered five above - appreciated stock or land deducted at fair market value to 30% limit.

Keeping this simple, if you gifted $40,000.00 of the stock to your church which operates as a tax exempt 501(c)(3), the church could sell the gifted stock at zero tax. Since that organization is listed on Publication 78 as a public charity, you would be allowed the claim the deduction on Schedule A, line 19. However, you will not be able to claim the entire $40,000.00 gift because the maximum you are allowed to claim on this year's 1040 is 30%. In this case, since the gift is appreciated stock, your deduction is limited to $30,000.00 because your Taxable Adjusted Gross Income was $100,000.00. If it was a cash gift, the deduction limit would be 60% of your TAGI effective 2018.

The great news is the IRS will let you carry forward onto next year's 1040 the unused $10,000.00 from this year. See Schedule A, Line 18 – carry forward from prior year.

This paragraph will be met with controversy. Current and deferred charitable giving is a balancing act of supporting worthy causes now verses making larger gifts later using charitable retirement planning strategies. This is a subjective decision for each person and depending on your circumstances, armed with knowledge, I am hopeful you will find the balance to use the tax code to your benefit and that of the causes you desire to see succeed. From my years of experience, those who do charitable retirement planning tend to make larger annual, substantial gifts to worthy causes because they have extra funds as a result of a well-coordinated tax plan. As you begin using Schedule A, line 19, it will take time to find your balance.

For this person above, he or she wanted to affect a current gift to a specific charity now. The remainder of this section will be focused on Charitable Retirement Planning using the deductibility chart at the beginning of this chapter. But first, let's make certain we understand the rules.

If you make $100,000.00 of Adjusted Taxable Gross Income this year, can you donate more than the allowed percentages listed at the beginning of this chapter to charitable causes or plans? Yes, you can. For example, if you made $100,000.00 this year, you could donate any amount you desire to a worthy charity. Can you legally donate $5,000,000.00 cash to a charity or charitable retirement plan? Yes, you can. However, using the 60% cash deduction rule (2018), the donor is limited to claiming a maximum of $60,000.00 this year. The unused $4,940,000.00 charitable gift can be carried forward to use over the next one plus five years on future 1040s. Some readers will say that is ridiculous. How can someone with a taxable income of $100,000.00 have that kind of wealth? Easy, they learned how to grow wealth tax smart and limit their taxable income. We call these people wealthy, not rich.

Many times, donors of major gifts cannot use the entire charitable income tax deduction. Some wait until late in their life to do proactive tax planning; others, start very early. Sadly, many advisors know how to use one model of the Charitable Remainder Trust, but there are several variations that accomplish many short and long-term goals. First, you need to know what your goals are. Next, you will need to find an advisor with a deep understand of the various structures that are available. Depending on the nature and character of the asset, your advisor will rank which structures provide you the desired benefits you seek based upon your goals.

Without question, consumers wait until the last minute to begin asking the right questions of the right advisors. If you are making money, be proactive and start asking questions about tax reduction and elimination strategies now. You probably invested tons of time seeking out the perfect investment, now that it is a success, you are caught unprepared for the tax exposure upon liquidation. Almost weekly I receive calls from investors who are at the close of escrow seeking a tax "Hail Mary" and that is not the right time. As a matter of control, if your objective is to avail yourself to maximum use of the entire Federal Code, you might need to implement some strategies two years and one day before the liquidation event for maximum tax benefit with certain strategies.

Chapter 12
The Charitable Gift Annuity
– One of my favorites!

If you are over age 55, you will probably fall in love with this extremely simple, but powerful tool – of which there are many variations to help you achieve multiple objectives. A Charitable Gift Annuity (CGA) is not an insurance product sold by your financial advisor. These are offered by licensed, qualified charities to issue these as contracts. I would speculate less than 10% of US Charitable Organization offer the CGA. This is not a trust or insurance policy. There are four parts to a CGA.

The donor (you) gift assets such as cash or appreciated stock to the qualified charity. A few charities can accept gifts of real estate. The charity issues to the donor a contract with an obligation to pay. The donor is considered the annuitant to receive said payments calculated on age, or term of years, etc. Therefore, this makes it a standard contract. The payout rates are tied to actuary tables established by the American Council on Gift Annuities (ACGA). To help govern this process and to protect the consumer, most state insurance commissioners will regulate and oversee this program. Here is where the fun part begins.

There are many ways to set up these CGA contracts. The most common is the Immediate One Life CGA. Mr. Smith donates $30,000.00 of cash to the charity in exchange for a CGA. The payment to Mr. Smith will be dependent upon a few variables. Since this is for his life and not a term of years (that is an option), his payout is based upon his age and the current American Council on Gift Annuities (ACGA) rate. At his age of 75, he is eligible for a single person rate of 5.8% using 2017 tables. Mr. Smith is in the 35% Tax Bracket and his life expectancy is 15.2 years. This means he will be able to claim an income tax deduction of $13,916.00. That deduction should generate for him approximately $4,871.00 in tax savings. Some of you at this point are thinking wait a minute, "Why did he not get to claim the full $30,000.00 deduction"? Unlike a Charitable Trust which is subject to Tier Four Accounting Rules, the CGA will make a distribution that is part return of principle and part taxable income. Since part is return of principle, there is no tax benefit for that portion of the gift. Hang on, the fun is about to begin.

Let's assume Mr. Smith had that same cash earning 1.2% at his local bank. As such, that $30,000.00 is producing a whopping $360.00 of new, taxable income for him. Because of his age and ACGA rate, the CGA will pay him 5.8% which is $1,740.00 of income, part tax free and part taxable. Question number 1. Who wants $360.00 a year for life and who wants $1,740.00 a year for life?

In effect, when you combine the actual tax savings and the income, in order for Mr. Smith to obtain an after-tax benefit of 5.8% using other investment opportunities, his financial advisor would need to generate a pretax rate of return of 9.7%.

Countless times I work with an elder seeking to protect their money from down side market risk and provide them a solid source of income. Often, they will have a testamentary charitable gift in their Will, Trust, Insurance or Quailed Plan to benefit charity upon their death. Whenever I see that fact pattern, someone has failed in their advisory capacity. If Mr. Smith died tomorrow with a testamentary gift in his estate plan to XYZ Charity, will he get to enjoy the whopper income tax savings? No. Will he sleep comfortably every night knowing he is getting $1,740.00 a year versus $360.00 a year? Yes.

Uneducated advisors are quick to chime in with "what if he dies in three years after doing the CGA"? Who cares? He was leaving a gift to charity upon his death anyway! Doing the CGA while he is alive, increased his income, provided him a current income tax deduction and he gets the satisfaction of increasing his relationship with his favorite charity.

At this point, I need to share a few pointers about advisor knowledge or conflicts. Since the bank and financial advisory firms cannot sell this contract or get a commission, how eager do you think they will be to share this strategy with you? Next, if Mr. Smith withdraws $30,000.00 from his bank account or brokerage account, the banker and financial planner make less money on their commissions and fees because it is no longer with them. In other words, you are taking bread off their plate. So be forewarned, it is very unlikely those advisors will recommend a CGA.

Since this is not a trust but a contract, your attorney does not make money. Your CPA is about the only advisor with a "dog in this hunt". He or she will get a 1099R from the charity administering the CGA fund and add that to your 1040 for reporting, which adds a few seconds to their time compiling your annual tax return. I will state, the CPA is probably the only advisor when it comes to charitable tax planning who can give you an unbiased opinion.

Again, the CGA is probably the most overlooked, under used planning tool in the country. And get this, you can start a Charitable Gift Annuity with as little as $5,000.00 or $10,000.00.

These can be set up for as Immediate, Deferred or Testamentary Annuities for yourself or others.

These can be set up with separate or joint property agreements for one or two lives. In some cases, you can add another person as a beneficiary of the income payout.

You can set these up for the benefit of other people, however; you may lose some tax benefits. The charity will make you aware of the state and federal tax issues. Many times, the CGA is still a worthy strategy without the tax benefits for the donor.

In other words, this is an extremely flexible tool. Now to share with you my favorite CGA for those still working, age 55 or older. I will use a single person to make this simple.

Mrs. Jones is an employee at a local law firm. She is 56 years young, divorced, with two adult children, and does not have access to a 401K. She has been faithfully funding her IRA each year currently at $5,500.00 in 2017, and she is very concerned her retirement years will have limited income. She has a Taxable Adjusted Gross Income of $80,000.00 after all deductions and she has been a great steward of her funds and has less than ten years remaining on her mortgage at 3.5%.

Mrs. Jones would like to contribute more to her retirement plan and somehow, reduce her taxes now. Although she is over 55, the last thing she needs now is higher taxable income. It would be wise for her to consider using a Deferred Flexible Charitable Gift Annuity.

Under this model, she elects to choose at a future date for the charity to begin sending her a check. She likes this flexibility of this plan because she does not know when she will be ready to retire, and she will get an income tax deduction upon funding the CGA this year. The funds in the CGA will grow over time, which can increase her future income payouts. Maybe next year she does a Deferred Flexible CGA for $7,000.00 at a different charity and maybe the following year she does not fund a CGA, but instead plans the vacation of a lifetime to Europe.

In other words, she has total control and at any point after age 60 (or whatever age the charity allows payout), she can call the charity and flip the switch "on" for income. At that point, minor adjustments are then calculated to determine her payout. Here is where a pile of technical, boring tax jargon would be inserted, but I promised to spare you those data points.

In this case, let's assume Mrs. Jones buys a Deferred Flexible CGA each year for $5,000.00 for the next ten years. That means, if she elects to retire in ten years, she could become eligible to start drawing some level of Social Security, she could start taking distributions (or not) from her IRA and she could direct the charity to start sending her income (or defer it longer). The key here is to understand that she now has access to three buckets of retirement income that she controls!

In this case, Mrs. Jones has an additional bucket of retirement funds to supplement her retirement life style, partly thanks to some wonderful income tax benefits from Uncle Sam. Granted, upon her death, her heirs will get a few hundred bucks from her social security bucket, the Traditional IRA will pass to them as taxable income and the CGA fund will go to those charities who underwrote the CGA.

The less educated advisor will opine the kids "got the shaft". Mrs. Jones had at least one smart advisor where she purchased a nice life insurance policy which will transfer to the heirs up upon her death, probably zero tax. Did I mention part of the life product was possible due to the income tax savings generated because of the CGA?

Too often in this country, we and our advisors fail to look at the big picture. Rare are the plans I see created in 3D format that will stand the test of time or factor in financial consumption by the client. It costs money for us to breathe, eat and live. We as human beings are consumers of our own wealth. Without sound tax advice, we will continue to overpay our income tax and retire in less style.

The primary reason I wrote this book was to help you reduce the amount of taxes you will pay for the remainder of your life. There are many boxes on a tax return, but it is up to you to use as many of those boxes that make sense for your short and long-term objectives.

If you are living pay check to pay check and you are in a very low-income tax bracket, tax planning is probably not your primary concern. But if you strive to learn proper budgeting, over time you will find yourself with tax issues.

Although I used very small sums of money to discuss the CGA, there is no limit as to the size of a CGA. Each CGA is separate, therefore, if you have nine CGAs, each one is independent of the other, even if all are at the same charity.

I have seen CGAs funded with more than $1M. Sometimes the CGA can produce better results than a Charitable Remainder Trust. It is always smart to compare them against one another.

This is how simple it is to set up a CGA. Call your favorite charity to make an appointment to set up a CGA. The contract is typically two pages or less. You make your choices about how you want the CGA structured (immediate, deferred, flexible, single, joint, or for someone else). The charity will often prepare you an illustration to demonstrate the who, what, when and how components. You write a check or transfer stocks to the charity and you get a letter for your tax deduction. No attorney, accountant, financial planner, banker or insurance agent is needed. Again, if you desire to speak to an advisor, go to a tax professional.

Today, many charities will have an interactive web site where you can use their on-line calculators with complete anonymity. You will normally find these calculators under their planned giving section.

Chapter 13
Blended Gifts – Part Sale / Part Charitable Gift

Are you tired of paying capital gains tax when you sell an appreciated asset such as stock or real estate? With proper planning, you can avoid paying that optional tax for the rest of your life.

A blended gift sale means the asset was divided prior to a tax trigger event. Before we explore how to use this very easy tax planning tool you must first understand there is a timing and procedural process that SHALL be an integral part of the plan. In Commissioner verses Ferguson of the IRS, 9th Circuit Court, No. 98-70095, decided April 07, 1999, a huge victory was handed to the IRS because of prearranged sale activities. If you are a code head, go do your research on this very important case.

For simplicity sake, this case defined the order in which you should position an asset prior to a sale if one of your objectives is to reduce or eliminate an imminent tax event. The best way to avoid violating this tax case is to meet with your tax advisor and attorney well in advance of any discussions with potential buyers before you discuss selling your business or property with a broker, or before any form of negotiations take place.

Many seasoned advisors will suggest you set up the tax reduction structure in advance of any form of prepositioning of the asset for sale. The key to surviving an audit where the IRS believes you have violated Ferguson is "What did you do first, second and third?" They look for the order, purpose and timing of the events which led to the transaction event. There is a large body of law and tax code which addresses this technical, but simple issue.

When I teach tax planning to business owners at professional events, I will make the following statement. If you are operating a business, you need to run that business as if it were for sale every single day. This should include discussing with your advisors your desired exit plan, which must address your future extremely large tax event whether it might be this year or years down the road. You should always be prepared for that unsolicited buyer who is ready to purchase on their time line – not yours!

Your goal is to sell your business at the highest price and our taxing authorities are hoping you get that result. If you want to pay the least amount of tax, you must proactively plan for that future event NOW! I promise you, your business will change hands one day either by sale, divorce, bankruptcy or death. You are the person in charge of your tax bill, not your advisors! Now let's have some fun selling assets with little or no tax – being ever mindful of Ferguson.

Think of a round, eight inches in diameter pecan pie that represents your business or appreciated asset. In this case, the pecan pie (publicly traded stock) will sale for $110,000.00. The basis (materials to construct the pie) was $10,000.00. The basis will not be taxed because you previously paid the tax on those funds.

The $100,000.00 gain will be subject to federal short or long-term capital gains, and depending on your state, it may be subject to some form of capital gains tax or simply converted into income tax; such is the case in California. It may also be subject to Net Investment Income Tax often referred to as Obama Care Tax. For the sake of simplicity, let's use 30% to compute the total tax. If nothing proactive is done to address this wealth destruction event, you will lose $30,000.00 in tax.

Strategy #1. If you donated the entire asset to charity and the charity sold the asset, it would be a zero-tax event. That gift would also generate a very nice charitable income tax deduction for you to apply on Schedule A, Line 19. In this example, gifting 100% of the stock will provide you a $110,000.00 income tax deduction and depending on your Taxable Adjusted Gross Income, you may claim that amount up to 30% of your AGI. If you cannot apply the full amount in one year, no worries, the IRS will let you carry forward the unused amount for this year plus five more years. If your objective was to make a tax efficient donation and secure a nice tax benefit, you are done.

Strategy #2. But what if you were seeking to sell the asset in such a way as to gift a portion of the pecan pie to a charitable retirement plan (Charitable Gift Annuity, Charitable Trust, etc.) but also take home a portion that would-be tax efficient (cash in your pocket)? Depending on your end of year Taxable Adjusted Gross Income, your tax advisor could run calculations to predict what percentage of the pecan pie should be contributed to the charitable retirement plan that would in effect create a zero-tax sale.

Consider this. Mr. and Mrs. Jones, both age 68, have an appreciated block of stock which has done very well. Unfortunately, all indications predict the stock will lose great value in the coming months. If they liquidate now, it will be a huge tax event. They decide to explore using a blended gift strategy to reduce their capital gain tax exposure, create a supplemental retirement plan, and reinvest the net after tax proceeds into a new stock with a new basis. This is an excellent plan.

In this case, they gift 60% of the stock or pecan pie to their favorite charity in exchange for an Immediate Charitable Gift Annuity (CGA) for Two Lives. The American Council on Gift Annuities rate for a Two Life, Joint and Survivor gift annuity is 4.4%. Their combined life expectancy is 27.8 years. If they contribute $66,000.00 of the stock to the CGA, the stock will be converted to cash with zero tax by the charity. Mr. and Mrs. Jones will receive an annual payment of $2,904.00 for life. Of that amount, $203.91 will be tax free return of principle up until their life expectancy in 27.8 years. If one or both continue to live, the charity will continue paying the survivor $2,904.00, however; upon reaching their life expectancy date (27.8 years), 100% of the payment to Mr. and or Mrs. Jones will be subject to taxation.

Mr. and Mrs. Jones will enjoy a $20,252.00 charitable income tax deduction. Their effective annuity payout rate is 5.13% when you combine their tax benefits.

In this case, $44,000 of the stock was personally sold which did trigger a capital gains tax event on this portion and possibly a state tax event. But thanks to a very large charitable income tax deduction, their tax liability will be significantly reduced. Again, had they desired to ZERO OUT 100% of the tax, they could have gifted a larger portion to the CGA or other charitable structure to accomplish this all too easy tax strategy.

Strategy #3. Similar to the Charitable Gift Annuity in Strategy #2, they elect to establish a FlipCRUT with a Net Income Makeup Provision. In this case, they desire to sale the asset with little or no capital gains tax exposure but would prefer to defer the income payout from the charitable trust to a future date. This method allows them to sale the portion in the CRUT Tax Free, obtain a generous income tax deduction now and since this is a trust, they plan to use it next year to contribute more appreciated stock to build up the corpus (principal) in the trust. Unlike the Charitable Gift Annuity, they cannot contribute additional funds into that contract. They could establish a new charitable gift annuity next year.

Both strategy #2 and #3 are somewhat similar in many respects, but there are several differences. Deciding which strategy is best is where that trusted and experienced advisor can help. Some feel charitable tax planning is complex and for the untrained advisor, that is true. Often, I speak at continuing education events for advisors and I will make the following challenge. If anyone can put a strategy on the table that can out preform what can be done using comprehensive charitable retirement planning, I will buy them dinner. I have never had to buy dinner for any advisor for that challenge.

The key to this level of wealth control is being proactive and having advisors who can help you explore all your options. I am the first to admit, I do not know everything. I have not met anyone who does know everything, but your odds of paying the least tax is done when your advisors work together as a team and invite experts from respective fields to assist with technical issues outside of their wheel house.

If you ask the right question to the wrong advisor, the answer is still wrong!

Whether it is a C Corp, S Corp, LLC, LP, real estate, stock, etc., if you plan to sale an appreciated asset or business, begin by identifying the tax exit planning first – years before the actual event. This will help guide the processes to improve your financial statements, goals and objectives.

Chapter 14
Better Than an IRA or 401K?
The Retirement Uni-Trust!

If you could fund more money into an IRA or 401K and get the tax benefits now, would you? Chances are your answer would be Yes! The ability to grow funds in a tax friendly environment for the purposes of retirement is a very powerful tool. Granted, as you grow those funds, the tax on those dollars are growing to benefit you and the IRS at the same time. But absent the IRA / 401(k) / Qualified Plan model, there are few, if any, effective tools where the bulk of America can invest dollars into a plan to provide for their retirement years.

In the sixties, these Qualified Plans were sold to Congress as Salary Reduction Plans to augment Social Security benefits for older Americans in the future. At that time, no one thought Social Security would become such as controversial or potentially, none viable program that might not be able to return funds back to its contributors down the road.

Over the past four decades, we have witnessed pension plans evaporating one after the other to the point where few are alive today. I retired from the US Air Force in 1998 and I do receive a small pension for those 20 years of active duty service. Before my death, I am certain Congress will enact law that will create an off set to whatever I paid into Social Security as a double dipper.

My wife Laura, a career school teacher and now school administrator is not certain the CA State Teachers Retirement System will survive. Both of our children, currently in their thirties, have great jobs, but no company pension is offered.

Declining pensions, evaporating pensions, no pensions, questionable Social Security, what can we do but fund our own retirement programs – BUT THE GOVERNMENT LIMITS OUR CONTRIBTIONS! Or do they?

By now, you know I am about to share with you another best kept retirement planning secret. Since Qualified Plans have a very low maximum funding threshold, it becomes obvious that if you contributed $5,500.00 a year into a qualified plan for twenty years, you would have $110,000.00 plus hopefully some compounding growth. Your financial planner, accountant and attorney all support you funding those types of plans because they are simple and frankly, about your only option to grow funds in a tax efficient, long term manner.

What if you make $300,000.00 a year as an employee?

What if you could fund far more money into a plan that grew in a deferred, compounding account like the qualified plans? What if the future distribution to you from that account could be subject to lower tax capital gains rates versus ordinary income tax? What if your financial planner, accountant or attorney did not know or even worse, had no experience with this powerful retirement tool?

Introducing the long time, been around for almost a century, huge body of proven tax law, better than an IRA, the Charitable Remainder Trust! It works for rich and not so rich people – like you. Before you close this book and your brain, you MUST get past the word charity.

First, on behalf of the IRS and your state taxing authorities, I want to thank you for your mandatory donations from the date you became a tax-payer / tax-donor! That's right, our tax system is designed to take funds from you then distribute that social capital (taxes) to programs, causes, etc., to support the common good of the nation.

Next, you must understand WHY our tax code provides such powerful retirement planning tools under the name of Charity. Imagine for a moment, your home town needs two soup kitchens to help the less fortunate. One soup kitchen will be operated by the government and the other by a not-for-profit charitable foundation. Both have the same size and type of building, same number of employees paid the same wages, both purchase from the same vendors the same amount of food at the same price, in other words, they are mirror organizations at every level. Here is your question. Which one is the least expensive to operate and provides the same solution to your community?

In fact, by a ratio of 2.7 dollars to one, the charity is literally saving this county far more money doing programs our government(s) should not be doing. Why, because the cost of government is out of control with budget deficit costs, fraud, waste, pork barrel, and the list of reasons our tax dollars become less effective grows. In fact, less than 30% of our tax dollars support something tangible. Thankfully, even our dumbest group of politicians understand that point and that is why the charitable part of our tax code continues to expand and provide powerful tools to bless you and your favorite causes.

Now to hurt your head. Imagine a married couple, John and Mary Smith, ages 42 and 40. Both are employees, two children, mortgage, and they make $312,900.00 a year as a computer engineer and surgical nurse. For this exercise, what if they could fund their respective Individual Retirement Accounts with $5,500.00 each for a combined total of $11,000.00 each year. Although they are probably over the maximum allowed income threshold to contribute to an IRA, give me some latitude to paint a comparison. That IRA Contribution did reduce their Adjusted Gross Income from $312,900.00 to $301,900.00. That saved them a little over $4,500.00 in combined tax. In twenty years, assuming they contribute the maximum amount they will accumulate $220,000.00 plus some compounded growth. I will forgo the discussion of the rate of return since every financial planner will argue the rate is too high or too low, but for the sake of this discussion, will you allow me to illustrate the IRA fund grew to an amount of $600,000.00? Regardless of whether the fund is $500,000.00 or $1,000,000.00, will that fund be large enough, along with their Social Security check, to survive? Chances are, no.

Let's get serious. Using this couple, what if they used a Charitable Remainder Uni-Trust (CRUT) as a retirement plan? The trust could be established to allow them to make future contributions of cash or appreciated assets at any time. Those contributions would be tax deductible, they would elect not to take a distribution from the charitable trust until a later date of their choosing, and the funds distributed from the charitable trust would be subject to the Four Tier Accounting rules instead of simply ordinary income tax rules like the IRA or 401(k). In other words, potentially preferred capital gains distribution rules.

Let's play with some numbers. With a combined taxable income of $301,900.00 (after funding their IRA) they technically could contribute 50% (2017) of cash to their CRUT. As such, if they could afford it, they could max out their Schedule A, Line 19 deduction to $151,950.00! The reality is no, but for the sake of teaching you what you do not know, hang with me.

Assuming they contributed $30,000.00 this year. That would save them another $13,000.00 in tax. If they funded both their IRA and CRUT, they would be setting aside $42,000.00 annual for their retirement. In twenty years, they would have $840,000.00 in principal and hopefully, a pile of compounded growth.

What if they funded their CRUT with $40,000.00 a year? Without question, the Charitable Retirement Trust will blow the doors of any qualified plan because it is not capped at $5,500.00 a year.

Remember, upon the death of John and Mary, the funds remaining in the Charitable Trust will be distributed to one or more designated charities of their choice. At this point, the untrained advisor will state the IRA was better than the CRUT. WRONG again! Upon the death of John and Mary, the Traditional IRA will be distributed to your other partner, your federal and state taxing authorities, then the remainder will be distributed to your heirs – now subject to their bankruptcies, divorce, law suits, etc. See Supreme Court Ruling on Clark v Rameker, 2014.

If you plan to live or die, fund the Charitable Trust and use a small portion of the income tax savings to buy a wealth replacement life insurance product. With proper planning, the Life Insurance death benefit will transfer to your heir's income and estate tax free.

I speak at many events to include continuing education for professional advisors. I tell them they need to use this strategy to reduce their annual income tax to retire in style. I tell them that if they elect NOT TO DO THIS, be sure and teach their siblings this concept in hopes their siblings will take them in when they run out of retirement money.

There are many types and ways to design and structure a Charitable Trust for your benefit. First, you need to learn the word charity is your best tax deduction friend. This is one reason the wealthy and famous use charitable strategies all the time. The next problem are your advisors. Unless you are their poor client which means they have many rich clients, chances are, they have little experience with this level of planning. In other words, if you have been complaining to your advisors about your tax liability being too high for years, they would have already introduced you to this very powerful planning tool – even if you do not have a philanthropic bone in your body!

I had a person tell me they had no ties to charities and felt that charities were a nuisance. But, he wanted to retire in style and needed far more than the limited qualified plan options could give him. I told him he could do a Charitable Trust to maximize his income tax benefits and simply name the IRS as the charitable beneficiary of the fund when he died. Suddenly, he thought of a worthy charity to name.

Closing comments. If your annual income is less than $100,000.00 and you are under 55, charitable planning may not pencil out on that one data point. When you begin a charitable trust with amounts as small as $30,000.00, the attorney, accounting and other fees will be a little steep to start, but after the fund has about $120,000.00, it will pencil, and you will be glad you did it.

A couple of drafting points for your attorney if he or she has limited or no charitable tax planning experience. First, tell them to co-counsel with someone who does charitable trusts as a primary part of their practice and next, ask them to discuss the 20-year payout option. Simply put, once the trust is created, that provision will cause the trust to be on the hook to payout to you, or your children, should you die within the next 20 years. For example, you and spouse fund the trust for the next 8 years and you both pass in a terrible car crash. The heirs identified in the trust would be the income beneficiaries for the following 12 years of payout.

Also, the financial advisor needs to understand his or her role as it pertains to the investments. Make certain they understand the tax nature and character of those investments as the taxation will flow through the charitable trust to you subject to the Four Tier Accounting rules. Again, would you prefer income subject to ordinary income tax rules or capital gains tax rules? Smart advisors know how to do this, which puts more tax smart money into your retirement pocket!

The trust will be an Irrevocable Trust where you are the grantor and funder. You will need to name a charitable beneficiary. I suggest you discuss reserving the right to change the name of that charitable beneficiary. Some charities will pay the attorney to do the charitable trust for you for free. If yes, ask if there is any language in the trust that mandates a portion of the charitable remainderman cannot be changed? Many of those types of FREE charitable trust will provide that a portion cannot be changed. Down the road, what if you part ways with that charity due to religion, politics, or whatever. They will still receive a portion of the charitable remainderman upon your death! For the cost to hire an attorney to prepare the trust to give the most options for me and for my family, I would write the check to my attorney!

Next, there are funding calculations called the five, fifty and ten percent rules. These are used to determine if the donor will be entitled to a charitable income tax deduction, what your maximum payout rate, and other technical attributes. Many attorneys do not know income or investment tax law. Your CPA should be involved before you hire an attorney to design the charitable trust.

If you desire to retire OK, fund the IRA. If you want to retire in style, get educated about the various Charitable Retirement Trust models and learn how to use that tool to do more than simply create a powerful retirement vehicle.

Otherwise, you have the right to do nothing, overpay your taxes and hope your relatives can take care of you down the road.

Chapter 15
To Roth or Not to Roth, that is the question?

This chapter will not be about slings, arrows or taking up arms against a sea of troubles. Instead, we are going to explore the age-old question, should I use a Roth or Traditional IRA for my retirement?

The next time you meet with your tax professional, banker or financial planner, ask them to show you the difference between the two. Let's have a little fun and establish some parameters to illustrate the point.

Let's assume you contributed $30,000 into both plans at the 33% income tax bracket. Yes, I realize there are limits based on age, AGI, etc., but hear me out.

Let's assume you will also retire in the 33% income tax bracket.

Let's use the same investment portfolio and advisor for both plans with a rate of return of 7.2%.

Let's illustrate the differences of these plans over a 10-year period. Which plan will outperform the other?

Is the Roth or Traditional IRA best?

Using the Traditional IRA (Pre-Tax) illustration it should look like this.

Gross Contribution:	$30,000.00
No Tax Withheld	-$0
Net to Invest	$30,000.00
Rate of Return	7.2%
Period 10 Years	x10
Tax Deferred Value	$60,000.00
Take Growth Out	7.2%
Pre-Tax Distribution	$4,320.00
Less 33% Tax Rate	-$1,425.00
Spendable Income	**$2,894.40**

Using the ROTH (After-Tax) illustration, it should look like this.

Gross Contribution:	$30,000.00
Less 33% Tax Rate	-$9,900.00
Net to Invest	$20,100.00
Rate of Return	7.2%
Period 10 Years	x10
Account value	$40,200.00
Take Growth Out	7.2%
Tax Rate	0%
Spendable Income	**$2,894.40**

From this exercise, when comparing apples to oranges, both appear the same. The real question to ask is not which is better than the other. Focus on issues like your current age, marital status, are you at the beginning or peak of your earnings career? Are you a business owner? Do you feel taxes will be more or less when you are ready to retire?

Many advisors will tell you that you will be in a lower tax bracket when you retire. Really, how poor do you want to be when you retire? Most of us enjoy the income we have prior to retirement and will most likely be accustomed to living that life style! When you and your spouse die, is it one of your goals to transfer wealth to your heirs as taxable or non-taxable monies? Will your estate become subject to estate taxes when you die? These are a few of the many questions to begin this very important discussion.

Here is my point. This Roth verses IRA decision should be made in front of a knowledgeable advisor who can help you explore your overall short and long-term tax and retirement objectives. My best advice for you is to stop gaining financial advice from the radio, TV or media, as most of those advisors are not licensed and literally are prohibited from providing legal, tax, investment or insurance advice.

All that financial pornography (marketing) is about getting you to put your money with their company, as they are advertising. To find wise counsel, ask friends, colleagues and your other advisors for a recommendation. Interview the recommended parties and start a relationship with the person you feel will invest and hopefully, safeguard your retirement nest egg.

Two, final points. If you are using an online account for your retirement nest egg, you may be shocked to learn you could have had a real person doing a better job for you for the same or less fee. It is shocking how many people do not know how to calculate what the actual fees are for their money under a computer managed account!

Lastly, I am asked all the time, should I fund any type of qualified plan? Or, should I only fund a plan if my employer does some form of match? I feel that once you have discretionary income and you are moving up the tax rate scale, regardless if the employer does any form of match, as long as there is a block on a 1040 which will allow you to obtain a current income tax benefit now, I would use it provided nothing else does a better job.

In the future, when you take funds from your deferred taxable account, there are many other strategies you can use to help reduce the tax bite on those accounts. If you are going to fund a tax deferred income tax retirement plan you must be willing to identify and incorporate tax reduction strategies when you take distributions from the plan. Otherwise, there is no real net benefit to using a taxable retirement plan.

Is the ROTH, IRA or 401(k) better? It depends on your objectives. Clearly, if you are in the same tax bracket going in and taking funds out down the road with the same growth, I proved technically is no difference.

Chapter 16
Will Your Traditional IRA Actually
Get to Your Heirs?

In other chapters I have mentioned that qualified plans now face a new threat upon our death. In 2014, in a landmark unanimous decision by the US Supreme Court, a ruling in respect to a creditors' bankruptcy claim finally tested the question: "Are inherited retirement plans afforded the same asset protections as the person who started the plan?" That answer is "NO". Your plan upon your death as it transfers to a non-spouse (individual), is subject to the creditor claims of that beneficiary.

In the Clark v Rameker case, the Supreme Court came to that conclusion focusing on two primary points. Did the IRA beneficiary establish the plan for their retirement benefit? In this case, mom created the plan. The second point was, who funded the plan? Again, that was mom and not the beneficiary (daughter). Therefore, the daughter did not create, nor could she have funded mom's IRA plan.

With those two points, the Supreme Court ruled an Inherited IRA is not protected with any form of asset protection and is subject to judgments, creditors' claims, etc., like any other asset. Here is the link to a short and easy to read court order regarding the ruling.
https://www.supremecourt.gov/opinions/13pdf/13-299_6k4c.pdf

Under current rules, when a qualified plan owner dies, the custodian may offer up to three methods for the non-spouse beneficiary to accept the distribution. The beneficiary may elect to take it all at once or the beneficiary may take distributions as five equal payments over five years. And the beneficiary may be offered to accept the IRA in the form of a Stretch Option.

In other words, the new IRA owner (beneficiary) elects for the custodian to make future Required Minimum Distributions (RMD payouts) based on the new IRA owner's current age or eldest beneficiary if more than one. In other words, a new calculation is made based on the beneficiary's age and the custodian, using a different IRS RMD table, and will make distributions – regardless of the age of the beneficiary.

The Inherited IRA owner does not wait until they turn 70.5 years of age, they start getting RMD distributions right away. The 70.5 years of age rule is for the person who created the IRA and funded the account.

Most IRA owners (Parents) wrongfully assume their IRA upon death will not payout until their children reach 70.5 years of age, but instead sit there as a bucket of money, when and if their children need it! Under the Stretch Option Plan, the new Inherited IRA owner will retain the right to raid the IRA fund at any time, but he or she will pay the tax on those distributions.

The Stretch Option is a very powerful election to grow funds for a beneficiary, however, we need to give thought to the asset protection issue addressed in Clark v Rameker since an Inherited IRA is now subject to the beneficiary's creditors and predators. Although losing IRA funds to a judgment is painful enough, the issue that really stings is "Who gets the 1099R when the IRA Custodian disburses out those funds to pay the judgment creditor?" That is a double whammy! The beneficiary gets to pay the tax on the money distributed from the account.

Welcome the Stand-Alone IRA Inheritance Trust. I love this trust when it is drafted by an attorney who truly knows the landscape of this powerful instrument. Keep in mind, about 80% of the Inherited IRA Trusts I have seen are frankly, "crap". One must really qualify the attorney who advertises that he / she can do this niche Trust.

Here are some of the reasons I love the Stand-Alone IRA Inheritance Trust. First, only mom and or dad can create it. If a married couple, each will establish a separate IRA Trust because we do not know who will die first. Also, since there are no married IRA accounts and IRAs are considered separate property - even community property states cannot get around the two Trust structure for a married couple.

Now that we know who can establish the Trust, it is never funded while they are alive, and the Trust is funded after death based on the IRA designated Beneficiary Form. The IRA Beneficiary Form may have a portion going outright to the child and a portion funding the IRA Trust. The client has full control of the IRA designated Beneficiary form and can change it every day.

The key here is how to use the Trust to provide the highest degree of asset protection considering the Clark v Rameker decision. There are four design models the client can elect for the attorney to draft the Trust. These choices revolve around who is the trustee, access to the principle, trust protector provisions and distributions. If the attorney you meet with states there is only one way to do this, you should seek another opinion.

You have many options for this Trust to be designed to accomplish your objectives. Watch out for that attorney who uses templates, as I have found the best attorneys avoid templates. I am a huge fan of the Wealth Counsel drafting system for attorneys and without question, the quality of their documents is superior to any drafting system I have seen to date. Although an attorney with this drafting system does not guarantee that he or she knows what they are doing. But, it does greatly increase the odds that the attorney is on the short list of great attorneys who could draft your trust very well. Go to www.estateplanning.com to find a Wealth Counsel attorney near you.

Here is why I love these tools. Although the IRA is a taxable distribution plan, if properly structured, it can be designed to force the stretch option to do the most good for the beneficiary. What if you have a child that spends money as fast as it lands in their hands? Or what if you have a child in a profession such as physician, attorney, contractor, architect and other professions subject to a higher degree of law suits? What if you have a child that has been married six times and he is forty-five years young?

These are great reasons to begin this discussion about your Qualified Plan. If not, if you have children like this, maybe you should give the IRA to charity?

Let's have some fun solving this problem. What if you structured the trust to preserve and protect the principle of the IRA allowing only the RMD to be distributed to the beneficiary? Using that model, a $200,000.00 IRA as seed money into the IRA Trust, over 30 years, will grow to over $2,000,000.00, while making its mandatory RMD.

Consider this. Since the bulk of Millennials do not and will not have a retirement pension, with proper planning, you could use this model to create an income stream that could act like a pension. I would also like to see a "Hail Mary" provision in the Trust that would allow the trust protector or trustee the power to distribute more funds as needed if the Required Minimum Distribution was insufficient that year. Research "Trust Protector" on Google. You will probably find a Forbes article stating why every trust should have a Trust Protector. I agree, I have one in all my Trusts.

If your children have done well for themselves and they do not need this taxable inheritance asset, what if you have named your grandchildren as the beneficiary of this trust? When you factor the small RMD payout percentage for a younger person, the growth and size of this Inherited Account could be huge in 40, 50, or 60 years. Remember, that money grows without a tax haircut and the only tax paid is on the distribution. Ask your CPA or Financial Planner to illustrate what an Inherited IRA would look like over 40 years for a grandchild. At first, you will not believe your eyes.

In summary, the rules have changed in respect to your qualified plan accounts when you die. In my opinion, planning for your qualified plans has become more difficult than drafting a trust for avoiding probate expense and disgruntled heirs.

If your qualified plan is over $300,000.00, you owe it to your heirs to seek well qualified professional advice. You can find several articles on the not so safe and true Internet and others that are wrong. I will give a shout out to Ed Slott. He is one of the few advisors who understands this complicated asset and tax strategy. His web site has many excellent articles about this topic.

Remember, only the IRA owner (creator) can do the above. Once the IRA owner has died, the above is not an option for the beneficiary to rescue the Inherited IRA Account.

One additional point in respect to Special Needs Beneficiaries. For many with medical needs, the use of a well-designed Special Needs Trust (SNT) can be a blessing after mom and dad pass. The purpose of the SNT is to provide a funding strategy so as not to interrupt or preclude a person upon an inheritance from receiving their government benefits. Your attorney can draft an SNT for immediate funding or in your revocable living trust as a testamentary provision for design, then funding.

The key to remember when identifying the monies or assets to fund the SNT is watch out for assets that trigger IRD such as a Traditional IRA or 401K. These are huge tax disasters because the SNT Trust is taxed at a very aggressive tax rate.

A few years ago, I worked on an estate plan where mom and dad had three children, one with severe disabilities currently on government support often referred to as a Medi-Medi beneficiary. Mom and dad were in their late sixties, their home was paid off, minor debts, $900,000.00 in a Traditional IRA, $100,000.00 in cash type assets.

For the SNT child, any direct inheritance would create some form of dollar for dollar disqualification of those medical and financial government benefits. The challenge here is NOT to fund any portion of the Traditional IRA into the SNT. Their objective was to leave a larger portion of the estate to the SNT child and the other two children were very supportive of that objective.

Since the bulk of the liquid assets of the estate are subject to income tax now or IRD tax later, and since mom and dad were in a relatively low tax bracket, it made sense for them to start stripping out funds from the Traditional IRA and converting those into a ROTH IRA. Using this model, mom and dad are now able to strip out and convert part of the Traditional IRA to a ROTH which now means, the ROTH can flow into the SNT without creating a tax disaster.

Over several years, they were able to balance the nature and character of their retirement assets in a manner that upon their death, will appropriately fund the SNT for the child with special needs and provide funds for their two other children.

Chapter 17
The "Give It Away Twice Trust"

Some people state, "When I am dead and gone, I don't care who gets what or how". That statement is one of the most overused, untrue statements a person with any level of financial means will ever express.

Granted, it is a great statement to act as a defense mechanism to postpone any meaningful discussion about your eventual demise, but the reality is, you probably do care. Since there are only four places your money will go upon your death, you will desire that most of your wealth transfers to your heirs and / or charity with the least amount of your wealth going to the government.

Considering the bulk of people who actually work to create their estates, most do care who does get what, when and how. Over a decade, I worked at a few estate planning law firms and discovered only a few estates have a remote chance of becoming multi-generational wealth transfers. In other words, due to poor planning, the transfer of wealth will last a short time period after the passing of the parents. In fact, studies show more than one third of estate beneficiaries (inheritance) had negative savings within two years. Another study suggested teenagers with an outright inheritance more than $100,000.00 had a new car within seventeen days. Clearly, estate beneficiaries of today are poorly prepared to receive even the most modest of estates from their parents. Think of this. Could each of your children properly handle their inheritance if you died today?

The reason I share this up front is to help you think through the process of balancing the inheritance in a way to protect your heirs from becoming a statistic like the two above. One planning method I love, which is gaining broad popularity, is addressing those two important issues. First, the Income in Respect of a Decedent (IRD) tax disaster from Qualified Plans and second, creating an income stream to provide for the heirs for up to a maximum of twenty years from your grave.

In Chapter Eleven, we introduced Charitable Tax Planning Basics. Here is another powerful method using a Testamentary Charitable Remainder

Uni-Trust (TCRUT). Simply, upon the death of the Qualified Plan Owner, part or all the qualified fund could be directed to a Charitable Trust that springs into effect by a written document such as a Will or Revocable Trust (normally second death planning). Let's explore an actual case I designed several years ago.

Tim and Susan raised four children. Tim passed away three years ago. Susan did not remarry. The estate was set up to provide for the survivor, then pass the entire estate to the children in equal shares, outright. The estate consisted of a paid off home valued at $400,000.00, cash and other securities valued at $400,000.00, and a Traditional IRA with $800,000.00. Susan had no debt and the estate was not subject to estate taxes. On the surface, most will say this is simple math. Since the estate is valued at $1,600,000.00, divided by four beneficiaries, each child's pretax share will be $400,000.00. Remember the IRA will be subject to income tax paid by the children at their respective tax rate.

Now for the rest of the story. Of the four children, two are strong money managers, one is borderline of being good with money and one child, well let's say he is of the creative sort who is expected to blow his inheritance in less than two years. Granted, some will argue this is a waste of time, but Susan is losing sleep worrying if the creative child will become a financial burden to the three other children after her death! Susan has every right to worry because if the creative child does blow his inheritance, it is likely he will become a burden to his siblings, potentially causing future social and emotional strife.

One suggestion Susan liked was to allow a small portion of the estate to pass outright to each heir. For example, $50,000.00 outright distribution at some point shortly after the death of Susan. Then, using the proceeds from the sale of the home and the remaining non-qualified monies, fund a Personal Asset Protection Trust for each child with separate EIN numbers, etc., would be funded. A lengthy discussion about who should or could act as the trustee for each sub trust could be inserted here taking up another ten pages, but not today. Clearly, the creative child should not be trustee of his trust.

Upon Susan's death, a portion of funds ($50,000) would be distributed outright, the remainder would be placed into asset protection trusts for each child - safe from their future divorces, law suits, bankruptcy, etc., and now we need to address the taxable IRA. Susan and Tim both have been very generous with their time and financial contributions to a few local charities. Sadly, when they had their estate plan created by their local attorney, no one discussed any form of testamentary gift to charity. Susan stated she and Tim wanted to do more, but their advisors told them their estate was too modest.

Thankfully, the existing Trust was an all to survivor trust which means, Susan has full control and ownership as trustor and trustee of the non-qualified assets. Susan also has the power to restate and amend the Trust in its entirety. Therefore, modifying the Trust to include the Personal Asset Protection Trust for the children can be easily drafted by a qualified attorney with the proper training and experience (a short list of attorneys qualifies to do this level of planning).

In respect to the Traditional IRA which has been rolled into one account, Susan as the IRA owner, can change the designated beneficiary form to whomever or whatever charity she chooses. In this case, Susan's attorney could be taught how to also modify the Revocable Trust to include provisions for a springing, Testamentary Charitable Reminder Uni-Trust (TCRUT). The TCRUT will accept the qualified IRA funds shortly after her death and make a payout to her heirs for a maximum payout period not to exceed twenty years (limited by Federal law). That was a mouthful.

Here is how this will work. The attorney adds provision to establish the Charitable Remainder Uni-trust naming her heirs as the Income Beneficiaries. Susan will also name the charities to receive the trust funds upon completion of the twenty-year payout. Susan also has the right to allow the heirs to name the eventual gift to charity as well in the event she does not want to name a charity now.

The payout income from the TCRUT to the heirs can be structured as monthly, quarterly, semi-annual or annual payments. Payments to the heirs are subject to the four tier accountings rules (taxable distribution). In other words, instead of the taxable IRA becoming a tax bomb as an outright distribution, or a five-pay plan over five years or a stretch option payout, Susan has basically created an income stream to benefit her children from her grave!

When Susan passes, the heirs will receive a nice distribution ($50,000.00 tax free), another part is placed into a sub trust ($150,000.00 tax free), protected from creditors, predators, etc., and the "tax bomb" IRA converted into the TCRUT becomes a small income stream producing approximately $10,000.00 of annual income for the next twenty years for each beneficiary (approximately $200,000.00 of value per child) subject to the Tier Four accounting rules.

Now here is the cherry on top. Assuming the trust money manager has a net six percent rate of return on $800,000.00 and using a five percent payout of $40,000.00 a year, upon completion of the twenty-year trust, a total of $800,000.00 of taxable funds will be distributed to her heirs and approximately $800,000.00 will be distributed to the charities of her choice when the trust is terminated.

In effect, she gave away the most taxable part of her estate twice, $800,000.00 of less taxable income over twenty years then $800,000.00 to charity. And yes, since the payout income is only $10,000.00 per year per beneficiary, she probably saved more income tax for each heir. The miracle here is recognizing how to address these IRA Tax Disasters with a pro-active tool to provide safe income to the heirs and a sizable gift to charity over time.

Susan was in tears when we explained the overall plan. She never imagined she would be responsible for creating a gift of $800,000.00 to charity. Through her tears, she mumbled, "If only Tim were here to see this"!

I need to give credit where credit is due. This strategy was taught to me by one of my mentors, Charles Schultz, Esq., Owner of Crescendo Interactive, Inc. of Camarillo, CA. He and his team are thought leaders in the charitable tax world. Check out their work on their web site www.crescendointeractive.com.

In summary. It is up to you to ask the right questions of your advisors. If you have any form of a qualified plan, ask, "What happens to these funds when my spouse and I die"? "What strategies do you have to reduce my income tax when I start drawing funds from these plans?" "What can be done to protect these funds transferred to my heirs from their law suits, divorces, creditors, etc.?"

Remember, you have the right by default to overpay your tax by doing nothing. Our compulsory tax system is designed for the government to win at your expense. You also have the right to pay the least amount of tax – if you make wise choices annually and in your estate plans.

Chapter 18
Income in Respect of a Decedent (IRD)

A better term would be "Income in *Disrespect* of a Decedent (IRD)"! There is nothing respectful when an heir must pay income tax on an inheritance. A decedent is a person who is no longer living, thus, when a person is a legitimate taxpayer has died, all his or her assets become the estate. Keep in mind, decedents still have testamentary legal authority by a Will, Trust or other writing the power to effect financial transactions after death.

Although deceased, that person, or better yet the estate, did not die. Someone will be required to file a final income tax return, notice the taxing authorities a tax payer has died, process the estate either through probate or trust administration and the list continues to grow. And then a final tax return may be required for the estate long after the person has died. Larger estates may need to file an additional tax Form 706. That is the form for estates more than $5,600,000.00 as of 2018, which has now doubled to $11,200,000.00 per person under the new Tax Cuts and Jobs Act.

So where does IRD fit into this process? The majority of estates will transfer to heirs with no tax due because of the Step Up In Basis rule. Assets such as real estate, stocks, and cash can transfer tax smart (step up) with little or no gain event. However, items such as retirement plan assets, qualified plans, profit sharing plans, SEP, Keogh, certain bonds, annuity payments, IRA distributions, unpaid interest and dividends, salary, wages, and sales commission are a few of the assets subject to IRD. In a nut shell, had the person not died, they would be required to pay the income tax upon recognition of those funds.

Let's look at one nightmare estate plan I reviewed years ago. Dad had died several years prior and mom did not want to hire an attorney to do a formal estate plan. Mom had added her daughter onto the Deed title for the primary residence to avoid probate as Joint Tenants with Rights of Survivorship. OK, that could work for Probate avoidance (an option but maybe not the best option). The home was valued at $300,000.00 and was debt free.

Dad had rolled his Traditional IRA (previously a 401k) over to mom as the beneficiary upon his death. The value of the IRA plan was slightly over $300,000.00. So, mom named her son as the beneficiary of the IRA. When mom dies, will the estate be distributed equally to both beneficiaries? In other words, will both children receive about $300,000.00 of value? The pre-tax answer is Yes! However...

By now you have figured out the daughter received the home zero tax due to the Step Up in Basis Rule. The daughter could sell the house the next day with zero tax due and put $300,000.00 into her bank account.

After the IRA Custodian has proof the IRA owner has passed and determined the legal beneficiary of the IRA account, if the son takes the full IRA distribution, he will add that distribution (IRD) on top of his personal ordinary income. Not only did the son pay IRD tax but pushed himself into a higher tax bracket on his personal wages.

Will brother and sister see the brilliance or unfairness of this plan? Will the son be unhappy with his new tax bracket?

Sadly, this is an example repeated far too often. In the old days, you would hire an attorney to prepare a Will or Trust and life was simple. Today, with the myriad of different types of assets, taxation and death transfer protocols, basic planning fails to encompass a total wealth transfer solution often sought by mom and dad. This also means attorneys and more particularly those on-line legal document preparation companies, who receive minimal tax training, fail to identify the IRD tax bombs when doing the Will or Trust. Remember, while you are alive, and breathing is the best time to solve tax disasters versus leaving these IRD assets to heirs who will have little legal or tax authority to address the death tax triggers on IRD.

Today more than ever, a single advisor cannot address every wealth transfer aspect created by your estate. It is your duty to force your human advisors to collaborate about your needs, choices and testamentary objectives.

Many consumers see collaboration as an expense. But in the case above, considering the IRD tax liability will clearly exceed $100,000.00 for the son, he is now forced into a post mortem tax planning scenario to try and reduce his new inherited tax burden. I am certain the son would have happily paid for good legal and tax advice for mom while she was alive to begin the process of addressing both the tax consequences of the taxable IRA and equal distribution of the estate plan – which is what mom thought she did. Yes, he could opt for a five pay over five years IRA distribution or Stretch Option for the IRA, but mom had far more opportunities to reduce this tax disaster.

By the way, you should review your estate and tax plan every three to five years or whenever a major event occurs such as death of a spouse, divorce, death of a beneficiary, a new marriage, admittance into a long-term care facility, or sale of major assets such as a business or real property.

Personally, I sleep better after I meet with my advisors to review where we are, where we are going and what will happen when God takes me off this rock!

One final note. If your estate is over the Unified Life Time Credit currently (2018) $11,200,000.00 per person and you have assets subject to IRD, be sure to take your heart defibrillator or your nitroglycerin pills when you meet with your tax team. The IRD assets can be taxed both as part of the taxable estate (40% Federal Estate Tax), then what is left over will be ordinary income taxable to your heirs. In California, that number can hit about 82% of total tax on IRD assets when your estate is too large. Again, if this is you, while you are breathing, solve this IRD tax disaster while you can. And yes, there are several ways to address this depending on your objectives, age, etc. You will probably pay some tax, but anything is better than 82% tax in my humble opinion. And yes, the tax code will permanently change forever!

Chapter 19
Qualified Plan Tax Strip Out

This is the scenario in 2017: The client was 65, and his wife was 62. They had one son, a successful physician in Florida. Dad was about to retire as Vice President of a Property and Casualty Insurance Company in the midwest.

The parents had done very well. Their estate was currently valued at $27,000,000.00. Of that $15,000,000.00 was made up of IRAs, Deferred Compensation, Defined Benefit, etc. In other words, a huge portion of the estate was considered qualified funds which upon death would be subject to Income in Respect of a Decedent (IRD Tax) and Estate Tax. Thankfully, by not living in California, the estate would save 4%, but since the estate was well over the combined Unified Life Time Credit for mom and dad ($10,980,000.00 in 2017) they are looking at multiple layers of Death Tax.

From the Form 706 (Large Estate Tax Form), the trustee will list the assets and value of the estate either based on date of death or alternate valuation date. For simplicity sake, we will use date of death.

Assuming mom and dad died simultaneously in 2017, the Form 706 will list the estate value at $27M. Subtract the Life Time Unified Credit of $10.98M and their taxable estate will be $16,020,000.00. Then multiply that by 40% and the estate tax will land around $6,408,000.00. The great news is that the estate has plenty of cash type assets held in qualified accounts. Therefore, settling with the IRS within nine months should not be a problem.

After that tax is paid, the son, who is in the maximum income tax bracket himself, will continue to lose additional inheritance due to the IRD rule. See Chapter 18 about Income in Respect (IRD) Tax of a decedent.

But before this scenario could play out, mom and dad found out their estate was literally going to their least favorite charity (IRS) and very little would end up in the hands of their son, they elected to proactively strip out the qualified funds over the course of the next seven years.

They explored pulling out $2.5M annually from the qualified plan. Granted, this does create personal income recognition on their 1040, but they also made sizable contributions to a charitable tax structure to help reduce the overall income tax event. Again, they did not zero out the income tax event, but the overall objective was to take this 78%+ tax bomb and convert it into anything that would create a smaller tax burden to the estate and their son.

In this case, by stripping out qualified monies over time and making sizable income tax deductible contributions to a charitable retirement plan structure, the overall tax cost was reduced to 26%. They also used some of the income tax savings to buy a wealth replacement life insurance product, which mom and dad could use as an additional source of zero tax retirement income or the death benefit could pass to their son zero tax due to the trust structure for the insurance policy.

The key here was mom and dad were made aware of the "tax bomb" before detonation! Somehow, over all those years of them building up this huge tax bomb, not one of their advisors mentioned what would happen upon their death to these qualified plans. Dad asked, why in the world did none of them tell me? My reply will sting a bit, but the only logical answer was the money managers did not want the goose that lays the golden egg to stop funding the plan. If you knew you were funding a retirement plan that would be taxed more than 78%, how much would you continue to contribute?

On a side note. Their successful son has a license to practice in a profession that tends to get hit with law suits. He is already over the $11M estate value himself, maximum income tax bracket and has been named twice in malpractice law suits. Thank goodness for malpractice insurance and asset protection structures.

More important to mom, dad and the son after the tax issues were addressed was how to protect the inheritance for their son from his future malpractice claims, divorces, etc. This too can be accomplished with proper planning by mom and dad while they are breathing and with legal mental capacity. Here, they explored an asset protection trust for their son. Upon their death, the estate proceeds drop into a trust for the benefit of the son. An independent trustee or other party will distribute monies to the son as needed, based on the language of the trust.

In this case, saving over $6M in tax was important, but also, making certain this large estate did not end up in the wrong hands was equally important.

Rule #1. If you lose an asset in a law suit, divorce, bankruptcy, or tax lien, you no longer have a tax burden. Always, protect the assets, create the tax problem, and then solve it before you create the tax trigger.

Rule #2. Due to the Clark vs Rameker Supreme Court (Unanimous) decision in 2014, assuming no tax or asset protection planning was executed by mom and dad prior to their death, their son would be the natural beneficiary of the qualified monies. Simply stated, funds held in inherited IRA accounts are not retirement funds. Which means, if the son becomes subject to a judgment, the inherited qualified funds are now subject to that recovery and guess who gets that tax bill when the plan custodian distributes the funds to the judgment creditor?

Rule #3. Regardless of the size of your estate, if you are going to fund a qualified plan, it is paramount you understand what tools are at your disposal to withdraw those future taxable funds with less tax exposure to yourself and how to transfer those plans (or the value of those plans) to your heirs with less tax and more asset protection. If your advisors look at you with a blank stare when you ask how to do this, you need to find better advisors!

Rule #4. If an advisor states it is wise to convert IRA assets into a Roth, ask why! Most do not know why and if you are in a high-income tax bracket, what tool(s) are you going to use to help offset that income tax event? Be very careful converting IRA funds to a Roth. If it makes tax sense, great. This is a tax decision, not a commission decision for your advisor.

Chapter 20
Business Owner Tax Credits and Additional Deductions (CCTC / NEC / WOTC)

There are several tax deduction or credit opportunities for qualifying business owners. This chapter will address the California Competes Tax Credit (CCTC), New Employment Credit (NEC), and Work Opportunity tax Credit (WOTC). Do these programs benefit every business owner? It depends.

Many states are creating tax and financial incentives to attract businesses and employers to their tax base. The objective is to attract businesses to create good paying jobs with excellent benefits.

In recent years, state governors began recruiting business owners from high tax states such as California, New York and others, with incentives to do business in their proactive, tax friendly, state. And it is working. With some state income tax rates above 12%, moving to a state with little or no state tax, combined with additional tax incentives to relocate your current business, is the new game in town or should I say country? I will speak in respect to California opportunities, but there are other states implementing similar programs to accomplish the primary goal which is to attract business and jobs to their state for the purpose of creating new tax payers and tax revenue. Parts of the following information was pulled from various State of California web sites. There is abundant data for your research.

California Competes Tax Credit (CCTC)

To complete with the loss of tax revenue, tax oppressive states like California are scrambling to slow down the exodus of businesses departing to greener pastures. One such program is called the California Competes Tax Credit (CCTC). This program was designed to replace the California Enterprise Zone program. The purpose of CCTC is to attract, expand and / or retain "high value" businesses growing in California with high economic multipliers to create good wages and benefits.

The amount of the tax credit award is dependent upon several factors aimed at helping the economic growth of the state. The key issue is not on proposed jobs and investment, but strong language from C level executives stating they "Will" relocate to another state in their application for the tax credit. Phase two of the award process may include the following in determination of an award.

- Number of jobs to be created or retained

- Compensation paid, including wages, benefits, and fringe benefits

- Investment in the state

- Unemployment or poverty where the business is located

- Incentives available to the business in the state (from all entities)

- Incentives available to the business in other states

- Duration of the proposed project

- Overall economic impact

- Strategic importance to the state, region or locality

- Opportunity for future growth

- Extent to which anticipated benefit exceeds the tax credit

- Supplemental financial or other documentation to verify information provided

As of 2016, twenty-nine companies were awarded almost $29 million in tax credits under the CCTC program. Although this is a great step in the right direction, only one third of the CCTC may be utilized by an S-Corporation to offset the tax on net income at the S-Corporation level (R&TC 23803 (a)(1) that first year of award and the unused two thirds may be carried forward. Clearly, this is another strategy that may or may not be a good fit for your company. To determine if your company is a good candidate, chances are your current CPA does not have the experience, technology or systems to determine what your potential credit award. Again, this is best calculated by a tax advisor who has an emphasis to practice in this area of tax. This is not the time for your CPA to spend hour upon hour learning about this credit at your expense and you become their first guinea pig. You should ask your CPA to seek out a professional who specializes in this type of work to run the numbers.

New Employment Credit (NEC)

Effective January 1, 2014 and prior to January 1, 2021, qualified tax payers who hire qualified full-time employees who perform more than 50% of that work in a designated census tract or economic development area, may be eligible for this program. Basically, there are parts of the state where there are high unemployment and high poverty areas. The objective is to entice business owners to create and keep jobs in those Designated Geographic Area (DGA). There are several ratios and calculations which are based on the number of prior year employees and proof of a net increase of total number of full-time employees working in California used in this process. Here are the Employer Requirements:

A qualified taxpayer:

- Is an employer engaged in a trade or business within a designated within a DGA?

- Is not engaged in any excluded businesses which are temporary help services or retail trades, and those primarily in food services, alcoholic beverage places, theater companies and dinner theater or casinos and casino hotels unless it is considered a small business.

- Is not engaged in a sexually-oriented business.

- Hires an individual that is a qualified full-time employee that works at least an average of 35 hours per week and meets all the following:

  - Is hired on or after January 1, 2014.

  - Performs at least 50% of his/her services for the employer in the DGA.

  - Receives starting wages that exceed 150% of the State minimum wage.

- Is paid hourly wages for an average of at least 35 hours per week, or is salaried, and paid for full-time employment.

- Meets one of five conditions upon commencement of employment (see below).

Employee Conditions

At the time of hire an individual meets any of the following conditions:

- Unemployed for 6 months or more, not having completed a degree or course of study.

  - Unemployed means: not receiving wages, not self-employed, and not a full-time student.

- Unemployed for 6 months or more, and completed a degree or course of study more than 12 months prior to hire.

  - Unemployed means: not receiving wages, not self-employed, and not a full-time student.

- Veteran, separated from the armed forces within 12 months.

- Recipient of the federal Earned Income Credit in the previous taxable year.

- Ex-offender convicted of a felony.

- Current recipient of CalWORKS or county general assistance.

Again, a key issue here is using qualified and experienced tax professionals to identify if this pencils out. Also, this program will require annual recertified to qualified employees. Does it work, yes, for the right business owner under these parameters.

Work Opportunity Tax Credit (WOTC)

The objective of WOTC is to encourage business owners to hire individuals who qualify as members of target groups and provide them with a federal tax credit incentive. Your first question may consist of "What is a target group"? As of 2017, a target group consist of:

A. Qualified recipients of Temporary Assistance to Needy Families (TANF).

B. Qualified veterans receiving Food Stamps or qualified veterans with a service connected disability who:

  − Have a hiring date which is not more than one year after having been discharged or released from active duty OR

  − Have aggregate periods of unemployment during the one-year period ending on the hiring date that equal or exceed six months.

C. Ex-felons hired no later than one year after conviction or release from prison.

D. Designated Community Resident − an individual who has attained ages 18 but not 40 on the hiring date who resides in an Empowerment Zone, or Rural Renewal County.

E. Vocational rehabilitation referrals, including Ticket Holders with an individual work plan developed and implemented by an Employment Network.

F. Qualified summer youth ages 16 through 17 who reside in an Empowerment Zone.

G. Qualified Food Stamp recipients ages 18 but not 40 on the hiring date.

H. Qualified recipients of Supplemental Security Income (SSI).

I. Long-term family assistance recipients

J. Not Used

K. Not Used

L. Qualified Long-Term Unemployment Recipients.

The 2015 Protecting Americans from Tax Hikes (PATH) Act Reauthorized the WOTC program and the Empower Zones. Certain target groups have a two-tier retention period for a minimum number of hours or days. The tax credit does vary, but it can be as high as $9,600.00 per qualified employee. If the employer cannot take the full credit amount due to their tax liability limitation, they may carry back one year, or forward for up to twenty years.

Key to successfully integrating this tax benefit into your business is hiring someone who does this type of planning as a profession. The list is a bit short, but again, if your CPA is not doing this type of work as a part of their primary services for their clients, you should ask them to help find that trained and experienced professional to determine if this program will financially benefit your business.

The bottom line of each of these programs is, does it make sense financially to the business owner? The objective of these programs is to create more jobs, which creates more tax payers, which in some cases, provides employment for persons who would otherwise remain unemployed or on welfare.

There are some minor additional administrative burdens, but when the systems are properly established from the beginning, the maintenance or recertification of employees is manageable and profitable!

Chapter 21
Game Over – End of Life

In 1789, Benjamin Franklin wrote a letter in respect to the new Constitution where he coined the phrase, "but in this world nothing can be said to be certain, except death and taxes". By now, if you have been reading this book, his statement about taxes may not be true for you.

In respect to the part about death, this book will not be able to change your outcome, but clearly, the point is made, that it is possible to have access to large income streams with minimal or no income tax, appreciated assets can be sold zero tax and large amounts of wealth can transfer to heirs zero tax – with proactive planning. To the untrained American, you see the tax code as your adversary, but once you learn how to fall in love with the tax code, your perspective will change, along with your outcomes.

Without question, your body will cease to function one day. At that point, depending on your marital status and state of residency, your estate will transfer in some form or fashion to other people, charities or to the government. You have the default right to do nothing about planning for that transfer event. The good news is that every state has a probate process to help estates transfer to the appropriate persons when there is no writing in place such as a Will, Trust or Pay on Death designation for your assets. Your county Probate Court, for a small nominal fee or "an arm and a leg", will process and marshal your assets to your intestate heirs.

Attorneys love it when you die without a Trust because many states have very generous rules to pay them well for their probate services. Even the court loves this process because they will get paid. And then there are the so-called beneficiaries. If there are plenty of assets, it is amazing how many people come out of the woodwork declaring they were promised they would receive a million dollars, the Lexus, the Rolex or whatever, by the decedent. Conversely, when you die broke and the funeral home needs to be paid, no one can remember your name.

After my retirement for the US Air Force and graduation from the Family Wealth Counseling program, I worked in law firms for twelve years. I was amazed to witness how often an estate was not distributed according to the decedent's testamentary wishes. There are many reasons for this such as: If there is no Will or Living Trust, if the documents are old, trusts were not funded, assets were not properly titled to the trust, designated beneficiary forms for life insurance or qualified plans were blank, second and third marriages not identified in their estate plan, documents prepared but not signed, missing pages from the original document, tax events not properly addressed, and the list goes on and on.

Contested estates normally arose from poor or no estate planning by the decedent. Additionally, great care should be considered when leaving a sizeable gift to someone who may not be able to handle money, or may be often flirt with law suits, has been married several times or has some form of drug or alcohol dependency. Furthermore, some heirs are in professions subject to law suits such as physicians, attorneys, contractors, business owners, etc. If the inheritance is distributed at the wrong time to the beneficiary, those funds could become subject to a judgment or creditors claim.

And yes, there are ways a trust can be designed to safeguard against all the above. Sadly, I have read more than 3,000 estate plans and the overwhelming majority of those documents are designed to simply avoid the probate process and expense. More on this later in this chapter.

The best advice is for you to meet with your estate planning attorney every three to five years, or upon the death of a spouse or immediate family member, a move to a different state, a major change in finances, major health events, heirs with health or financial difficulties, major tax or probate law changes, and sometimes simply to verify your wishes are still the same.

I was asked to review a trust while other advisors were discussing a financial planning issue with mom and dad. While I read the document, I noticed a name as a beneficiary of the Trust which was not a biological child of the Grantors. I interrupted the meeting and asked who this person was, and I knew I had asked a bad question immediately as the mother looked at me with eyes filled with hate. She stated, "Why do I need to know anything about that %$#*@?" I responded, "It appears she is not a biological descendent, but there is a provision to give her $75,000.00 upon the second death". Her face became ashen.

Dad immediately intervened and said she was the ex-wife of their son who divorced thirteen years ago. Needless to say, they had forgotten to review the trust after the "knockdown, drag out" divorce and remove that provision. The estate planning attorney was hired on the spot!

The bulk of estate plans tend to dispose of the inheritance as an outright distribution after taxes, administrative and other fees are paid. Although easy to write, that type of distribution comes with risk. Over the years, I watched beneficiaries lose their inheritance for a variety of reasons, all of which could have been avoided had the trust kept the funds in a springing sub-trust for the heir's benefit using the Health, Education, Maintenance and Support distribution rules. Simply stated, since the funds remain within a sub-trust and have not been distributed, provided the document has been drafted properly, those funds could be protected from a creditor or predator.

Most inheritances are lost under the following scenario. The estate or trust makes the inheritance distribution outright to the heir. The beneficiary takes the check and deposits it into the joint checking account. At that point, a form of transmutation has occurred making that property, depending on the state, jointly owned property.

The next day, the divorce papers arrive, and fifty percent of that inheritance is now in the hands of the ex-spouse and their new lover!

Had the parents elected for the funds to remain in trust, it would look like this. The Trust Administration attorney would establish the sub-trust and acquire an EIN number from the IRS. A new bank account would be established in the name of the sub-trust using the EIN number. The Trustee would direct the distribution of funds by having a check prepared in the name to the sub-trust. Then the funds would be deposited into the sub-trust bank account or brokerage account for the benefit of the beneficiary. At this point, those funds are sole and separate property. The trustee of the sub-trust can distribute the funds according to the terms of the trust.

For example, the beneficiary would like a new home valued at $500,000.00. The beneficiary selects the home and reports that information to the trustee. The trustee buys the new home in the name of the sub trust and the beneficiary and his current spouse live in the home. Three years later, a divorce is filed. What happens to the house owned by the trust? Nothing. It is an asset of the sub trust – not subject to divorce, law suits, etc. There is a bit more to this asset protection strategy, but this design is worth its weight in gold if a divorce occurs in the future for the beneficiary.

As you can see, keeping funds in trust for the benefit of heirs should be considered as a planning tool for their protection and the protection of the inheritance. Once inherited funds are lost, they are gone forever.

I make the following statement practically every week. If you lose an asset to a law suit, divorce or bankruptcy, you no longer have a tax problem. Always understand the level of asset protection you do or do not have, before it is too late to protect it. Once you are served with a notice of pending litigation, it is normally too late.

Here is an easy exercise to complete right now. You and your spouse (if applicable) die today. Get out your estate plan, read through the distribution scheme. Next, determine what assets are titled to the trust and what assets are outside of the trust, for the assets titled to the trust, this is simple. Next, as you determine what and when the trust is going to transfer and to whom, does it all make sense? Will the inheritance survive, will it help or hurt the beneficiary, and will it be taxable to the heir or the trust?

Next evaluate what happened to the assets outside of the trust. For assets such as qualified plans and life insurance, those plans would have a pay on death (POD) beneficiary designation. Those assets, once the plan administrator has evidence of the owners' death, will distribute according to the terms of that beneficiary form. Again, who will be the beneficiary of those assets, does it make sense, will it be taxable (Qualified Plans = YES), who will pay that tax and when?

If your estate is subject to estate tax, that tax bill is due within nine months of the date of death (last to die, if married in most cases). What will the tax bill be? What assets have been identified to pay that tax bill from the grave? Will payment of that tax bill interrupt the plan of trust or estate distribution? Has the tax bill been properly coordinated within the context of the overall plan? More often than not, families fail to plan for estate taxes.

With so many people designing their estate plans, establishing a business entity, and doing their taxes on the Internet, we are going to see a huge increase in the number of contested probates and estate administrations in the coming years. With such an abundance of information on the Internet, rarely will you find pages on wisdom. I love the Internet but considering the number of estate and tax disasters I have witnessed over the years, using the Internet is not going to provide you with the design specific to you and your objectives. You may save a few bucks on attorney or CPA fees, but I can assure you, those savings will most likely be pennies compared to poor tax and wealth transfer decisions you make on the Internet absent professional advice.

Questions to ask at every advisor appointment.

If I die today, what happens to my asset(s)? Will it be taxed?

Will this asset(s) be exposed to the creditors or predators of my heirs?

If you do not like their response, your next question is "How do we correct that issue"?

That face to face meeting with these tough questions are crucial. Estate and tax planning is about finding good advisors and building a relationship of trust.

Chapter 22
Summary – Call to Action

At this point, pull out your 1040 Tax Form and review it from beginning to end. If you do not understand it, ask your tax professional to explain it in layman's terms. If you have exercised every beneficial tax opportunity provided in our 77,000 pages of Federal Tax Code, your tax liability should de minims. If you are not satisfied with the results of your report card, now is the time to gather your advisors and have a meaningful discussion about their continued services for you.

I am hopeful you learned from this book that no one advisor can do it all! Clearly, it takes a team of highly motivated and educated advisors to help you pay the least amount of tax. Many advisors are in the business of providing you services based on what they want you to buy. I get it, people need to make a living, and many are scared to step outside of their box and into the world of tax. Because of this, you may need to do some searching to build a team to accomplish your goals.

By default, our governments have designed a beautiful compulsory tax system which they want you to use. You have the right to overpay your tax and you have the right to pay the least amount legally possible. If you do not like their default method, they are not going to show up on your door step, hold you by the hand and spoon feed you information on how to pay less tax. This is an "us" versus "them" environment because they think all your money belongs to them. Remember, they print the money and desire for you to have temporary use and ownership of said money.

I also believe you should ask for a second opinion on your investment portfolios, insurance, tax returns and estate planning documents every three to five years. If you are receiving top level services, a reputable advisor will tell you to stay on your path.

Now that you are armed with many tax secrets made simple, keep more of your money by paying less tax for the rest of your life!

I am hopeful you will apply this book and begin the process of reducing your income tax by 30-60% for the remainder of your life. Remember, tax reduction or tax elimination planning is a pro-active process. You must get off your butt to make it happen. If it was easy, you would already be doing it!

If you are NOT using Schedule A, Line 19 for maximum benefit, you will over pay your tax and retire poorly.

Before making any tax decision, you should always consult with a tax advisor.

Questions to Consider.

Look at last year's tax return. Compute how much you could have funded into a charitable retirement planning strategy, the income tax deduction and how much income tax you could have saved.

If you are living pay check to pay check, do you have a budget that works?

Do you have six months of emergency cash reserves?

Ask your advisors to show you how to reduce your income tax exposure by up to 60% per year.

Ask your advisors to show you how to by-pass, defer or possibly eliminate capital gains taxes when selling appreciated assets.

Ask your advisors to show you how to protect your assets from creditors and predators (lawsuits).

Ask your advisors to show you how to transfer wealth to your heirs safely.

How much is too much?

How much is too fast?

Ask your advisors to show you how to protect your heirs' inheritance from their divorces, lawsuits, bankruptcies and tax liens.

If you are funding a qualified plan, ask your advisors to show you how to reduce the tax on those distributions when you retire.

Ask your advisors to show you how much your qualified plan can distribute annually, while keeping abreast of inflation, when you retire at age?

Will your social security and taxable retirement accounts provide enough income to support your future lifestyle?

Have you heard a radio or television personality, posing as a financial planner, state you should never purchase cash value life insurance? Do you understand why that is most likely false? Why do they suggest that blindly?

When you purchase cash value life insurance, do you understand why it is a powerful "use it while you are alive zero tax income strategy" verses a death benefit? Most insurance agents do not know how to explain it either!

Recognizing Schedule A, Line 19 as the most powerful income tax deduction and retirement planning opportunity, why have none of your advisors shared this secret with you?

If you are a business owner, you MUST operate your business from the perspective it is for sale every day. If you were approached today with a fair purchase offer, what tax smart exit strategy could you use to pay the least tax? BTW: Business owners who FAIL to identify and implement a tax smart plan well in advance of that offer will discover minimal, if any, tax smart options can be used because of Commissioner v Ferguson.

If you are a business owner, are you fully utilizing the Qualified Business Income (QBI) to your benefit?

Are you meeting with your tax professional before end of year to address and correct what you could have done better to reduce your tax?

Made in the USA
San Bernardino, CA
23 September 2018